Mini-Society

Experiencing Real-World Economics in the Elementary School Classroom

Marilyn L. Kourilsky

University of California, Los Angeles

Addison-Wesley Publishing Company

Menlo Park, California · Reading, Massachusetts
London · Amsterdam · Don Mills, Ontario · Sydney

About the Author

Marilyn Kourilsky is both an economist and an educator. Her teaching experience has included the elementary and secondary levels. She is currently a professor in the UCLA Graduate School of Education and is the Director of Teacher Education. She has written seven books and over fifty articles, and has received numerous honors including the Outstanding Teacher Award from UCLA. Dr. Kourilsky resides in Encino, California with her husband and daughter.

This book is published by the Addison-Wesley Innovative Division.

Design by Colleen Hench
Illustrations by Corbin Hillam

Copyright © 1983 by Addison-Wesley Publishing Company, Inc.
All rights reserved. Printed in the United States of America.
Published simultaneously in Canada.

ISBN 0-201-20034-1
ABCDEFGHIJKL- ML -89876543

Dedication

In loving memory of Charles Lederman who epitomized the creativity and entrepreneurship that motivated the development of Mini-Society.

In honor of Mrs. Ruth Lederman who was his life-long inspiration.

Acknowledgments

I would like to especially thank Ellen Goldman Ortiz and Darlene Wilson for their special insights and contributions to Mini-Society. I also would like to thank the following individuals who have offered their ideas, time, and special inputs to strengthen and enrich the Mini-Society instructional system: Barbara Barclay, Garry Diamond, Paul Dunleavy, Lory Furse, Karen Gilbert, Edna Graff, Susan Gumelli, Nancy Jensen, Lucy Nye, Douglas Miller, Bonnie Meszaros, Jim O'Neill, Joan Perlof, Karen Sklar, and Doris Stevenson.

Special recognition should go to Greg Kourilsky, whose patience, encouragement, and intellectuality have all combined to make this a better book. And to Shari, because of your participation in Mini-Society, I now know what it is like to be a Mini-Society parent.

It is also my pleasure to thank Chevron USA Inc. for the first California financial support for Mini-Society workshops.

Finally, it is my pleasure to acknowledge the extensive support of the Charles Stewart Mott Foundation, whose generosity funded numerous workshops and other dissemination activities throughout the United States.

CONTENTS

PART I

INTRODUCTION

CHAPTER 1

AN INTRODUCTION TO THE MINI-SOCIETY INSTRUCTIONAL SYSTEM

Don has fallen victim to one of the occupational hazards that often confronts ten-year-olds—his teeth are crooked. So Don and his father visit the orthodontist. Much to Don's relief, only a retainer will be needed; much to his father's relief, a retainer is considerably less costly than a full set of braces.

After the diagnosis, the orthodontist takes Don's father aside to discuss the finances of the rehabilitation project. "We have a deferred payment program that is designed to minimize the burden on you," he says. "The price for the work on Don's teeth will be one thousand dollars, payable in four two-hundred-fifty-dollar installments that will begin in three months."

Don looks up from his Superheroes comic book and makes a counteroffer. "My dad will give you a check for nine hundred fifty dollars today."

The incredulous orthodontist reddens, then blusters, "What kind of kid is that? I don't think I even want to work on your mouth—it doesn't need to be any smarter!"

Don, composed and self-assured, then goes on to explain to the orthodontist that it's to his advantage to get nine hundred fifty dollars as soon as possible and invest it at the current rate of interest. Says Don to the perplexed orthodontist, "Didn't anyone ever teach you the time value of money?"

"Another gifted child story," you say. "I've heard a hundred just like it." No, Don is not a child prodigy. He is a perfectly average and representative member of a classroom Mini-Society where all the voting citizens are under twelve years of age. Don and more than 300,000 compatriots in Mini-Societies throughout the United States are the vanguard of a new breed of elementary school alumni. Incredibly enough, these youngsters understand more about the glue that holds our economic and political system together than most of the adult population.

There's no magic involved—no sleight of hand that transforms your thirty scruffy/adorable, dull/bright, exasperating/lovable individual personalities into instant tycoons or presidential candidates. Mini-Society is an instructional system that is being implemented successfully by thousands of teachers across the country with children that represent every socioeconomic level and ethnic background. These teachers have found that by following some specific initiating steps they can guide their students through the systematic formation of their own microcosmic society.

Cost-benefit analysis in the third grade? Not only possible, but imperative. Every year a new crop of young people leaves school and formally enters the ranks of adulthood. Whether they have officially graduated or have left without diplomas in hand, these people will encounter many circumstances and expectations for which they may be unprepared. They will begin to make individual life decisions that, in the aggregate, affect us all. They will be expected to participate in our economy as workers, consumers, savers, and investors, although the vast majority of them are economically illiterate and lack consumer awareness. They will be eligible to vote and expected to exercise their franchise intelligently and seriously; however, many of them are without a true understanding of our basic political processes. They will be expected to support themselves and select or prepare for a career in which they will participate for much of their lives, yet an astounding number do not know how or where to begin this process. These same young people will enter into interpersonal relationships that will have lasting effects on their social and economic lives, yet many of them lack practice in communication and other skills necessary to mature exchanges. Several of these young adults express strong convictions concerning political, economic, and moral aspects of life but have adopted these convictions without an in-depth examination of the underlying values they attempt to defend.

It is sadly clear that thirteen years of school have left a vast number of people unprepared to participate purposefully and knowledgeably in the basic roles they play in life. This is not to say that school has left them totally unexposed to the concepts involved in the real business of living. For example, every student has been required to study aspects of our governmental structure and political process. Some may even remember the facts they have learned; however, this collection of facts has little to do with the exercise of adult responsibilities in coping with the real world. These students may "know" about life in that they have digested certain concepts and facts, but they are lost when it comes to applying these facts to their own situations: in a sense they are functionally illiterate. Certainly we have all attempted to deal with this problem in a variety of ways, but teachers are rarely able to make essential economic concepts seem important and relevant enough to motivate students to learn them and apply them in real life.

I am convinced that the root of this functional illiteracy is the lack of opportunity to practice applying the knowledge that schooling attempts to impart. In order to learn in a functional sense, children must *do*. In the Mini-Society approach to instruction, learning by doing is the crucial, pivotal element. The Mini-Society instructional system is a self-organizing, experience-based approach to teaching youngsters about economics, government, career options, consumer issues, and values clarification. This learning-by-doing approach is the most effective way of teaching economic, governmental, and other concepts, and the children love participating and are, therefore, highly motivated. And you, the teacher, will be happy to know that it's operationally simple. You become facilitator and advisor while the students generate their own desire to learn concepts. Mini-Society's inherent exposure to experience causes participants to understand firsthand what it is they don't know and to seek out information for their own here-and-now benefit and reward.

The experiential path to learning—a natural route. A highly motivating instructional system, the Mini-Society encourages independent, creative, self-directed inquiry learning by the student with guidance by the teacher. Mini-Society has produced dramatic success in classrooms across the country. The students in these classes represent a full range of ability levels, geographical areas, and socioeconomic groups. The common element in the attainment of impressive cognitive and affective results was the use of the specific experiential approach that Mini-Society represents.

The Mini-Society approach to experiential learning builds upon three essential characteristics. Students must participate in experiences that provide:

1. Personal as opposed to vicarious involvement.

Mini-Society students are not analyzing problems that occurred in the past. They are experiencing personal involvement in a living society, the form and operation of which they have created. Dilemmas that require decision making and action are their personal and societal dilemmas. Analysis and decision making become much more interesting and vital when it is the students' own lives they are discussing.

2. Active as opposed to passive roles.

Mini-Society citizens are not simply reading about experiences, nor are they being lectured on an abstract situation or subject. They are mentally and physically moving about. When problems arise and decisions must be made, the students are not given prearranged answers. They are actively involved in the analysis of their own problem situations and in the selection of the alternative actions through which they can resolve problems they face.

3. Opportunity for decision making, the consequences of which they will bear.

The decisions that students make in Mini-Society will not be authoritatively judged as "right" or "wrong," nor will their decisions be overturned by an authority who foresees consequences that the young decision-makers haven't anticipated. Mini-Society students make decisions concerning their individual career or business lives and their societal operations with the understanding that they will live with the situations their decisions create. If individuals decide they are not happy with the results of decisions they have made, they are responsible for making changes in their lives to correct the unacceptable situation. If the citizenry is discontent with the results of a group decision, it is their responsibility to reanalyze the situation and adopt what they think will be a better alternative. Learning by doing in Mini-Society does not involve just any participation, but it involves a very specific kind of participation. It requires that students participate in experiences that are *personal* and *active* and that they bear the consequences of their analysis and decision making.

It is also not sufficient that students simply participate in the experience. The experience must be followed by *debriefing* (discussion) and analysis of the situation or problem they have just undergone.[1] Most of you played Monopoly as children, but probably few of you learned an extensive amount of economics from participating in the game. Yet it is entirely possible to learn several complex economic concepts through participation in Monopoly. Why doesn't playing the game usually result in this learning? Because most people do not have the opportunity (or the inclination) to step back from the play for analysis aimed at deriving the concepts they are seeing in action. They simply want to "experience"; that is, they want to play, and preferably win, the game.

The Mini-Society approach requires that students always experience a situation *before* they are assisted in analyzing the concepts. It is essential to learning that students constantly debrief and analyze in an inquiry-oriented discussion group in which your approach is nonauthoritative. Mini-Society is not based on learning because the knowledge "is good for you" or because it is something one will need to know later in life. Once the children have experienced a situation they are eager to analyze and learn about the concepts they have encountered. They are anxious to participate in a serious exploration of the alternatives available to them and to acquire the various skills that may help them cope with a situation. The students' fascination with concepts usually foreign to children their age is based on the perception that they need to know these ideas and acquire these skills *now* as opposed to an indefinite time in the future. Serious concern with their decision-making processes is grounded in the realization that they are involved in the real business of life rather than in hollow exercises of the intellect. Their decisions actually matter in the here and now. Within Mini-Society they control and shape their own future.

---

[1]The specifics of debriefing will be presented in Chapter 9.

The effects of Mini-Society participation have been measured and observed in classrooms around the country. Children of every background learn, apply, and retain economic concepts usually reserved for college sophomores. In fact, they often out-perform the college students on the depth of their understanding of some of the key economic concepts.

Dramatic changes also occur in the affective domain. Mini-Society participants display a heightened sense of self-esteem, an increase in assertiveness, a willingness to take logical economic risks, and more positive attitudes toward school and learning. They also exhibit realistic conceptions and understandings of adult roles as workers, consumers, savers, investors, and voters. Positive side effects of Mini-Society have been observed, with many participants showing an increased interest in reading and math, higher math and reading standardized test scores, and improved school attendance.

In this book you will find all the information you will need to initiate and maintain a Mini-Society in your classroom. It includes a basic background in economic concepts, which—perhaps to your surprise—you'll see is eminently understandable. If this is your first brush with the official vocabulary of economics, you will probably find that, although you didn't call them by name, you have been applying such concepts as opportunity cost, demand, and cost-benefit analysis to your own life for years.

The three chapters on "Getting Mini-Society Started" will explain your responsibilities as teacher in initiating the Mini-Society, the responsibilities of the students, and the ways in which money can be infused into the system. As the teacher, you will have the following responsibilities in generating the Mini-Society:

1. Focus on classroom scarcity situations.
2. Organize the students into an interaction–discussion group to resolve the scarcity situation.
3. Promote decision making and closure in selecting an alternative for resolving the scarcity problem in your classroom Mini-Society.

The students' responsibilities will be to:

1. Identify the activities for which they will be paid.
2. Name their Mini-Society country and currency.
3. Select the currency denominations they will use.
4. Decide on job criteria for civil servants and select people to fill the positions.
5. Choose a design for the Mini-Society currency and the flag, selecting from the ones submitted by the Mini-Society citizens.
6. Choose a form of government (if they decide a government is necessary).
7. Select a treasurer.

At this point your Mini-Society will be ready for the first receipt of income, and you'll move through the next six steps:

1. The winning currency design is drawn on the ditto or mimeograph masters.
2. The money supply is printed.
3. You turn the money supply over to the treasurer.
4. The treasurer supervises cutting the currency into individual bills.
5. The treasurer transfers the appropriate amount to each paymaster for the first day's payroll.
6. Paymasters deliver the first day's wages to their constituents.

You'll notice that at the end of each of these sections there is a chronological checklist. This allows you to quickly review the procedures and be sure the class is ready to proceed to the next step.

Once your Mini-Society has generated money into the system, it will begin to move into action with financial exchanges, the formation of businesses, and the dilemmas that confront the members of any economic system. Each of these areas will be covered in detail, and included are procedures for dealing with occurrences that have been found to be nearly universal in past Mini-Societies. In the event that the Mini-Society is not going quite as smoothly as hoped, procedures are presented that will help move it along.

The section on debriefing presents the substance and importance of the interaction–discussion group. During these sessions you and the children will discuss the events that have occurred in Mini-Society. The debriefings will run the gamut from economics to politics to government to law and will include the consideration of value judgments, differing points of view, and various alternatives.

The final portions of the book give you some added nuts and bolts: fables for amplifying some of the economic concepts and instructions on how to handle some of the mechanics of banking. There is a summary and review of the whole Mini-Society process, to which you may want to refer for an overview (Chapter 13), and Appendixes covering instructional materials and evaluation methods.

Add to the above procedures and guidelines your own brand of creativity, your particular style, and the uniqueness of your students, and you've got a flourishing society—one from which both you and your students can gain knowledge, insight, and much enjoyment.

PART II
GETTING MINI-SOCIETY STARTED

CHAPTER **2**

GETTING MINI-SOCIETY STARTED: THE RESPONSIBILITIES OF THE TEACHER

A.   Introduction

Your initial role as teacher in Mini-Society is that of intensive facilitator. Specific steps are presented through which you can arrange the impetus for the students' formation of their society. During the initial steps of getting it started your role will be most intensive. However, once you have accomplished your three responsibilities and helped guide the students through *their* six responsibilities in getting their Mini-Society started (Chapter 3), as well as assisted with the first receipt of income (Chapter 4), your role will alter and diminish. The teacher-intensive period of getting Mini-Society started rarely lasts longer than three weeks. After the initial period you are debriefer, private citizen, and maybe profit-making businessperson.

While getting it started you must take special care to guide the society's formation but not mold its shape. It can be a great temptation to steer the students toward a society that closely resembles your utopian ideal.

Your first decision in the implementation of Mini-Society concerns scheduling. The system is usually implemented during the social studies time period, so there should already be some time available for the insertion of Mini-Society into the school day. A time period of thirty-five to sixty minutes per day is advisable, at least three times per week for a minimum of ten weeks. Some teachers have successfully inserted Mini-Society into time slots usually reserved for language arts and arithmetic because of the heavy emphasis on these subjects, which usually arises as the children begin to run their own society; however, most teachers prefer to use Mini-Society as a basis for social studies and career education. The placement of Mini-Society during the school day entails determining which thirty-five- to sixty-minute period to select. Many have found it preferable to hold Mini-Society immediately following lunch or recess because it is an activity in which the students are physically active yet are involved in academic learning. A second reason for the after-lunch-or-recess placement of Mini-Society concerns the likelihood of food-oriented businesses developing when "Moving Mini-Society Ahead" (Part III) begins. Some snack items may be sold during the business operation of Mini-Society, and placement of the activity after lunch or recess usually insures that the children have at least had the opportunity to ingest some food of their family's planning before succumbing to the temptation of snacks.

B.   Objectives

After completing the activities in this chapter students will be able to:
1.   Recognize the dilemma of scarcity by defining its components and verbalizing that there is not enough of everything they want.
2.   React to the scarcity situation in the interaction–discussion group by offering tentative solutions to the problem of scarcity (e.g., first-come, first-served; need, etc.)
3.   Give an advantage and a disadvantage for each tentative solution to the scarcity problem.
4.   Select and defend at least one method of dealing with scarcity in the Mini-Society.

C.   Three Responsibilities of the Teacher

1.   Focus on Classroom Scarcity Situations

This is the first step toward a self-generating classroom economy. Scarcity is the central economic problem of all societies, and the Mini-Society citizens must truly feel their relationship to this ageless difficulty. Faced with scarcity (limited resources in opposition to relatively unlimited wants), societies evolve economic systems to allocate or distribute the scarce resources. So, too, will students, acting as a small society, generate a system to cope with the fact of scarcity as soon as they are unavoidably faced with the dilemma through some very real personal examples. Some children are already aware that there is often not enough of the things they want; others have not yet had to deal seriously with the fact. Almost none have approached the problem analytically in searching for resolutions. For example, in one upper-middle-class community, students were read a fable in which a magician provided the children of a make-believe land with all the toys they wanted. One child in the class yelled, ''Just like us!'' In communities with lower socioeconomic status it may be easier for the children to accept the existence of scarcity. They are well aware that the solution to a lack of desired goods is not simply a matter of going to the store to buy more; but to some students buying more at the store may seem an obvious and reasonable solution to scarcity problems.

To focus on classroom scarcity you should select a classroom item or items in which the children are extremely interested, or create a scarcity situation around an intrinsically motivating item. An example of initiating a relevant scarcity situation is to set up a new learning center or interest center with space for only a few children at a time. Do not include a time limit in the directions, and arrange for only one group at a time to use the center. You could then sit back and let the students realize the scarcity of space or time at the learning center. One Mini-Society teacher did this by bringing in a several-hundred-piece birdcage—disassembled. He created an interest center in which the students could assemble the birdcage at their own pace. The project was so popular that soon students approached him anxiously saying, ''But Bonnie has been at the center too long. When is her turn over? Make her give us a chance!'' The teacher allowed the situation to continue for a short time, commenting, ''We seem to have a problem, don't we? We seem to have a scarcity of time at the new center. Can you think of any solutions?'' When at least half the class had not only noticed but also had become concerned about the problem, the teacher went on to bring the class members together to discuss the problem.

There are numerous ways to focus on scarcity, and you are the best judge of which ones will be most effective for your particular grade level and group of students. You may wish to use one, two, or more of the following suggestions or to create your own scarcity situations. The main point is to focus on a scarcity situation that will be meaningful enough to your students that they will be eager to resolve it. The ideal approach to focusing on scarcity would include at least one activity from each of these two types: a classroom experience in which the students are faced directly with the scarcity of a desired item; and one in which the experience is more passive and vicarious to reinforce the concept of scarcity.

Suggested methods for focusing on scarcity. The following are examples of some of the situations that past Mini-Society teachers have devised to focus on scarcity. You may wish to use some, though not all, of these suggestions.

a.   Shortly before a holiday you can create an acute shortage of some art supplies. For example, before a Valentine's Day project you might have only four sheets of red or pink construction paper. Most of the children will simply not stand for blue or green hearts!

Also before some important art project you might "discover" that crayons, scissors, or other supplies are extremely limited. This is most productive if the particular situation makes sharing quite burdensome.

b.   You may create an enticing learning or interest center in which all the children wish to participate. One such center has already been described. Again, it is important that participation time for each student is *not* limited by posted rules and that space *is* limited so that only two or three students can be accommodated at a time. Particularly successful centers have provided opportunities to listen to popular music or story tapes (tapes should be lengthy, or several tapes should be available so students do not leave the center too quickly); play with various building material such as plastic brick sets, toy logs, or interlocking spools (there should be numerous pieces so that complex, time-consuming projects can be attempted); and complete a complicated puzzle (sometimes the children who have completed a puzzle have been allowed to keep it).

c.   If your school custodian agrees, you might arrange to have some of the furniture "disappear" for several days. When the children arrive at school one morning, there would be five or six fewer chairs than usual. Before this is attempted, you should be certain that there is an inconvenient but still viable alternative seating arrangement so that the scarcity situation does not intrude too much on the rest of the teaching day.

d.   You may provide a treat that is in very short supply. This is particularly successful if students have just finished a story such as *Charlie and the Chocolate Factory*. (Dahl, Roald, author. New York: Alfred A. Knopf, Inc., 1964). You could provide about five chocolate bars and ask the children for help in deciding who gets them. For even more emphasis, one chocolate bar could contain a Gold Certificate entitling the bearer to an ice-cream cone at the local ice-cream parlor. The presence of the certificate allows the students to understand some facts about sharing (which will undoubtedly be suggested as an allocation strategy); the difficulty of sharing an indivisible resource will become concrete reality. For example, in one class students decided to allocate their scarce resources (an ice-cream cone) on the basis of sharing. Most of the students seemed content with this decision until the sloppiest child in the class called out, "Dibs! I get the first lick!"

e.   You might create a scarcity of spaces available on an exciting field trip. This is especially successful if the location has great popular appeal (an amusement park), or if sample goodies will be included (such as in a trip to a cookie factory).

f.   For a vicarious activity you may read the children the scarcity fable concerning the kingdom of RumTumTum[1] and follow the accompanying discussion outline. The fable and discussion allow the children to experience an imagined scarcity situation. The fable lesson also does a marvelous job of reinforcing the concept of scarcity after it has been introduced through more personal active experiences.

g.   Another activity entails the use of any of the simulation games and inquiry lessons in which the children help a group of mythical people make decisions on limited resources. In these lessons the people are sometimes stranded on a desert island or lost in space and must decide what limited supplies they would choose to have.

Immediately following the introduction of classroom and vicarious scarcity situations you may wish to reinforce the concept of scarcity by having the children complete the scarcity worksheet included in Appendix 1, and/or initiating an assignment in which the children draw pictures of scarcity situations (the pictures then can be displayed on the bulletin board).

2. **Organize the Class into an Interaction–Discussion Group To Resolve the Problem of Classroom Scarcity**

Regardless of the particular scarce classroom items on which you choose to focus, it is important that the students be guided to resolve the scarcity problem and to live with their solution. When about half the students have become aware of and concerned about the problem being caused by scarcity in the classroom, you should call them together into a discussion group to deal with the problem.[2]

Once the group is convened, ask the students to verbalize the problem with the learning center (or crafts supplies, scissors, candy bars, etc.). The initial responses of third through sixth graders will be something like this: "Bobby is hogging the scissors" or "I never get to use the learning center, because I don't finish arithmetic fast enough." It is important to have students generalize the problem(s) enough so they realize and actually announce that there is "not enough" of something they want. The teacher can then give this situation its economic label: *scarcity*. You should introduce the word *scarcity*, or reinforce the name of the problem if the term *scarcity* has already been introduced. Scarcity is a *limited* number of resources (things we want to have or use) versus a greater number of uses of the resources than units available. At this point the students may tend to think of scarcity as a limited number of "things" overshadowed by a larger number of people who want the things. In the problem-solving discussion that follows, and in subsequent discussion, you should focus on the fact that a person may want more than one unit of a resource; *scarcity is really limited resources versus realtively unlimited wants or uses for the resources.*

Once the children have defined the problem as a scarcity problem, you can then help them in the discussion group to explore methods of allocating scarce resources. This can be done through brainstorming and/or role playing.

---

[1]Kourilsky, Marilyn. *Understanding Economics: Overview for Teachers, Experiences for Students.* Addison-Wesley Publishing Company, Menlo Park, CA. 1983.

[2]In some cases, there is no need to formally convene a discussion group, as the students are already gathered together in a discussion. For example, if the teacher has chosen method (d) as one way to focus on scarcity, the students are already in a group to help the teacher decide who will get the candy. If the teacher has chosen a method such as (b), the students have been experiencing scarcity within the regular operation of the classroom. These students will have to be called together to start the discussion of resolving scarcity.

*a.   **Brainstorming.*** The students should be asked to generate ways to resolve the scarcity situation they are facing; that is, they should think of ways to allocate (distribute) the scarce resources. They will suggest the same solutions that adults would (and that societies have), but they will state the seven- to twelve-year-olds' version of these classic allocation techniques. You will undoubtedly receive suggestions as shown in the Allocation Strategies Chart.

Allocation Strategies

Adult Version	Children's Version
1. First-come, first-served	"We could have a race" or "The first one in his seat after recess (or in the morning) gets _____ (the scarce resource)."
2. Lottery	"We could put all our names on little pieces of paper and put them in a box (or a hat or shoe) and draw to see who gets _____."
3. Need (or a specific criterion for need)	"We could give it to whomever would be happiest with it."
4. Planner decides	"You (teacher) could decide who gets _____." (Or, more rarely, if you have a relatively self-governing classroom, "Jenny can decide.")
5. Force	"You go out of the room and we'll decide who gets _____" or "We could have wrestling matches to decide."
6. Share	"We could divide _____ up into equal parts and we each get one piece."
7. Market mechanism (paying for the scarce resource with something of value.)	"Isn't there some way we could work to get part of _____ by sort of buying it?"

*b.   **Role playing.*** If the students have difficulty deriving allocation devices, you may prompt them by using examples of these allocation strategies from the real world or by using role-playing situations in which the students act out the allocation methods. For example, the game "musical chairs" may be played. At first, the chairs should be allotted on the traditional first-come, first-served basis. Then the rules should be altered so the last chair is allocated by lottery. Each time the game is played, the rules—the way the last chair is allocated—should be changed.

Once the students have generated various solutions to their problem of scarcity, they should discuss the advantages and disadvantages of each method. You should elicit the advantages and disadvantages from the students themselves by asking, "Is there anyone who doesn't like using this way of deciding who gets the scarce resources? Why don't you like it?" Examples of the advantages and disadvantages students usually identify are described in the following chart.

Strategy	Advantage	Disadvantage
First-come, first-served	Good method if (1) you are a fast runner or (2) you're a person who gets to school and can be in your seat first.	Unfair for people (1) who aren't good runners, such as someone who has a broken leg, or (2) whose parents take them to school on their way to work and always get there after the kids who ride the bus.
Lottery	Good if you are a lucky person who wins things.	Some people aren't lucky. ("I *never* win contests or *anything*.")
Need	Good if you are a person who is picked as needy.	You might think you need the resources, and others may not think so.
Planner (teacher) decides	Good if the planner likes you or if the planner is always "fair."	The planner (teacher) isn't always fair!
Force	Good for the strong people.	Not fair for people who aren't physically strong or who are smaller than others.
Share	Everyone gets an equal part. No one goes without.	(1) Not everyone wants some of every resource, and sometimes we want more than others do; (2) some resources can't be divided up; (3) sometimes an equal sharing might mean that no one gets enough.
Market mechanism	Great if you are able to earn some income (can get a job).	Not good if you can't find work or don't have any good business ideas.

To this point you have guided the students through the following progression:
- Students have been faced with actual scarcity situations within the classroom.
- Students have convened in a discussion group to define the problem they are facing (scarcity).
    - In the group, students have identified the possible solutions to their problem (e.g., they have identified allocation strategies.)
    - In the group, students have discussed the advantages and disadvantages of the allocation strategies they have identified.

When students are aware of the possible solutions to their problem and the advantages and disadvantages of each solution they should actually select a method for distributing the scarce items on which you have focused. This selection is usually best accomplished through voting, with the majority determining the strategy to be used. For each scarcity situation the students should select and experience an allocation strategy. They should then have the opportunity to express their reactions to the strategy. In a classroom where you have generated several scarce items, it is possible that students will select a different allocation strategy for each item. This activity will give students a chance to live through their decisions and experience the concrete reality of solutions they previously understood only in the abstract. For example, if you have focused on scarcity by using a popular learning center with no time limit and five chocolate candy bars for a class of thirty, the students might first deal with scarcity at the learning center. Perhaps they have elected to allocate time at the learning center through a lottery method. Depending on how satisfied the individuals are with lottery, they may or may not elect to trust luck for the allocation of the chocolate bars.

   c.   Special considerations for the discussion of allocation strategies. You should try to play devil's advocate in discussing all alternative allocation strategies. In discussing lottery, for example, you might say, "Is there anyone who never wins at contests?" There will always be one child who answers, "You bet!" The students, especially the younger ones, are likely to first present the alternative of *sharing*, because they have been socialized to provide that response. They may feel it is the response they should make or the one you want them to make. When discussing this alternative, make the students aware of the following facts:
   (1)   Some resources are not divisible and therefore are difficult or impossible to share. The example of musical chairs or a piece of bubble gum may be used to illustrate this problem.
   (2)   Sharing as a "good" thing is a value judgment. Although we often think of sharing as a positive action, it may be important that some things belong only to the individual. Wanting something for one's own does not necessarily make one a bad person. There are times to share and times when we don't want to share.
   (3)   Most importantly, the act of sharing assumes that *someone* had property rights (that is, owned the thing) to begin with and decided to share this property. The example of toys or a candy bar shared with siblings or friends may be used as an illustration here.

The alternative of allocation by *need* also raises some important considerations. It is essential that students realize that "need" is a value judgment; it is subjective. What one person believes is a need others may think of as a frivolity, which is why economists refer to "wants" rather than "needs." Students in one Mini-Society classroom were discussing the allocation of a scarce resource (candy), and some suggested allocating by "need," saying that skinny people needed the calories more than fat people. One rather plump boy could not accept the underlying assumption. "I'm not fat because I eat a lot," he maintained. "This is a glandular condition!" To illustrate the point, you might ask the students to decide what they would need if they were stranded on a desert island. Ask them to name the first ten items. They may agree on the first three (perhaps food, water, and shelter) but will probably have trouble agreeing on the rank order of these. Even if they easily reach consensus on these, it will be difficult to reach agreement on the other items that follow.

When discussing the alternative of having the planner (or teacher) decide, students may be wary of hurting your feelings, or they may seek to ingratiate themselves with you by choosing this alternative. Students may still be at the stage when they believe that teachers are superbeings. You may indicate that although you try to be fair, it isn't always possible; tell them that you are a human being with the failings (and also the *rights*) of other people. A statement such as the following can dispel illusions of perfection: "If I were the planner, I would give the scarce resource to the smartest students."

Regardless of the allocation method being discussed, the class should realize that there are always tradeoffs. There is no perfect solution.

Up until now, students have met in an interaction–discussion group to define the problem of scarcity, identify possible resolutions to the problem, discuss advantages and disadvantages of possible solutions, and select temporary solutions to isolated problems of scarcity. This procedure of resolving problems through an interaction–discussion group will eventually be used in Mini-Society in a number of ways: to provide students with economic, business, career, and consumer knowledge that the entire class can use to enhance their personal Mini-Society activities (e.g., when to change one's employment); to clarify values questions with respect to problems such as responsibility for public goods (e.g., who cleans the hamster cage); and, using the session as a town meeting, to resolve political and legal issues that arise in Mini-Society such as whether to have a government and, if so, what kind.

3. Promote Closure to Select an Alternative for Resolving Scarcity in Mini-Society

After you believe your students have had a sufficient opportunity to discuss, and in many cases experience, the advantages and disadvantages of the various allocation mechanisms around which economies are formed, you are ready to move to the next step. Remember, you still are "the teacher" and have not, as of yet, truly moved into your role as citizen and consultant. You should now challenge the students to form their own classroom society—to build a country that will operate fairly and smoothly and that will be a happy place to live. To get their society started, they must begin with some form of economy. I suggest you have them start with a market mechanism to facilitate exchange. You should make it clear that as their economy evolves they have the right to modify their economic system in any way they want.[3] At this point (not sooner) you can begin to move away from your role of authority figure to that of citizen and consultant. You will be explaining that future decisions in the society are the province of the students; however, you are still one citizen in the group. In a way you are their elder person of state and as such have knowledge from which students may benefit. At each meeting of the

---

[3]Your alternatives here are similar to those facing the teacher who wishes to introduce the mathematical concepts associated with representing and doing arithmetic with numbers expressed in various bases (base 16, base 10, base 8, base 2, etc.). The natural pedagogical path is to introduce the basic concepts in the context of the base 10 number system with which the students are already familiar. Once the students have acquired the fundamental principles underlying the base 10 number system, they are in a much betterposition to transfer this understanding to other based number systems. They will also more readily appreciate why other based number systems might be more appropriate or useful in different contexts (e.g., bases 2, 8, and 16 for computer applications). Similarly, your students have lived in a market economy and are at least casually familiar with how it operates. They will more readily grasp the basic concepts of economics if they are introduced to them in this familiar context. Once they have acquired the basic conceptual tools of economics, they will then be in an intellectual position to explore solutions other than the market system.

interaction–discussion group you should sit in a different location of the circle so that students do not identify an authority location or "front of the room." This will encourage the students to make their own decisions and will underscore the statement you will make that the society the students are about to create will truly be theirs to run in any manner they wish.

Upon reviewing the checklist at the end of this chapter, you are ready to move on to the next stage of getting Mini-Society started: the responsibilities of the students. If you have lived through stage one, you will especially enjoy stage two where you fall from impenetrable authority figure to mere mortal.

D. Checklist for Getting Mini-Society Started: The Responsibilities of the Teacher

The teacher can best determine if students are ready to move to the next step by consulting this checklist. If the following items have been accomplished, it is time to progress in the initiation of the classroom society.

1. Have you focused on classroom scarcity situations?
   a. at least one active, personal scarcity situation directly affecting the lives of the children _____
   b. at least one passive, vicarious situation to reinforce the concept of scarcity _____
   c. completed a scarcity worksheet (see Appendix 1) to reinforce the concept of scarcity _____
   d. discussed and defined the scarcity situations _____
2. Have you organized the class into an interaction–discussion group to:
   a. brainstorm and/or role play various allocation strategies to resolve the scarcity problems? _____
   b. discuss the advantages and disadvantages of each strategy? _____
   c. experience the method(s) selected? _____
   d. review the possible resolutions to the problem of scarcity? _____
3. Have you promoted closure in selecting an allocation strategy by:
   a. reiterating the advantages and disadvantages of each allocation strategy? _____
   b. introducing the concept of building a society in the classroom based on a market mechanism? _____
   c. reminding students that they may later alter their market mechanism? _____

Upon the election of some type of market solution for resolving the problem of classroom scarcity, the students are ready to assume their initial responsibilities as discussed in Chapter 3.

CHAPTER 3

GETTING MINI-SOCIETY STARTED: THE RESPONSIBILITIES OF THE STUDENTS

A. Introduction

You should initiate the second phase of "Getting Mini-Society Started" by assembling students into their interaction–discussion groups and indicating that there are several decisions necessary to getting their society started. This chapter focuses on the basic decisions the students must make and actions they must take to have a flourishing Mini-Society. Some groups of students may have additional suggestions you will want to use. For organizational purposes, the responsibilities of the students are presented in six distinct parts, although these tasks and their surrounding discussions frequently overlap.

As the students begin to assume their responsibilities in getting the Mini-Society started, you should be sure that parents are apprised of the method and purpose of Mini-Society. The materials section of this chapter contains a sample letter you may wish to modify for your use. Once the economy is on its feet you may wish to hold a parent orientation meeting. This should happen about three to four weeks after beginning the program and will be discussed in more detail in a subsequent chapter.

B. Objectives

After completing the activities in the chapter, students will:
1. Decide upon the activities for which they will be paid.
2. Decide upon the name of their country, and the advantages and disadvantages of particular denominations (an odd denomination bill might hamper efficient exchange because of the difficult computations that would be necessary.)
3. Decide upon the criteria for selecting civil servants (including paymasters, the treasurer, and the money cutters) to monitor or carry out activities associated with Mini-Society.
    a. Provide a rationale and priority for each criterion associated with a particular job.
    b. Create a job application form for civil servants in general or each job separately.
4. Fill out civil servant job application forms (if interested) and verbalize to a committee of three why they should be hired (i.e., special attributes they possess).

5. Discuss the advantages and disadvantages of various methods of submitting bids for the design of the currency and select one method from among the following:
    a. An individual student may submit a bid for any denomination of the currency.
    b. A group of individuals may submit a bid on any denomination of the currency.
    c. Students will form specific committees, and each committee will be assigned one denomination of currency to design; the best design from each committee is submitted to the "government," and the entire committee shares the fee for the winning design.

C.   Six Responsibilities of the Students

1.   Identify Activities for Which They Will Be Paid

In order for money to enter the system, students should decide on a limited number of activities for which they will be paid. These should be activities in which everyone can participate with goals that everyone can accomplish. They should be stated in operational form and limited in number (three or four is optimal) to avoid confusion in record keeping. The teacher should resist the temptation to intervene and decide, but should encourage the students to be fair.

Why infuse money on the basis of accomplished activities? The initial infusions of money into the Mini-Society could take several different routes. Why, then, has the preceding alternative been selected as the most appropriate? Largely it has been a process of elimination. Mini-Society could start with everyone automatically receiving an equal amount of money; however, this gives children an incorrect impression of economics. We are not born to parents having equal amounts of money, and we usually do not receive money for doing nothing. Or Mini-Society could start with the teacher randomly dispersing money in packets containing different amounts. This, perhaps, is more realistic, as we are born into families with different income levels. However, at the developmental stages of Mini-Society students, "random" is an abstract concept. The children may understand intellectually the explanation of randomization; yet there is a chance that some children who receive smaller bundles of money will blame themselves or feel that you have given them less money because of personal dislike.

In the earlier years of Mini-Society's development, the approach had been to deduct money for negative behaviors rather than pay for positive behaviors. The positive approach has not only proved more successful for independence of the students but also is more valid psychologically.

What are the major pitfalls at this decision-making stage? The major pitfall may be the temptation on your part to use this payment of money as a form of behavior modification. Perhaps you dislike students chewing gum in class. It may seem relatively harmless to pay students for not chewing gum in class. Behavior modification has been a much-discussed and debated issue in recent years. It has proved to be very effective under certain circumstances; however, among the major goals of Mini-Society are the development of decision-making skills, the development of a more internalized locus of control (i.e., a higher level of autonomy), and the acceptance of responsibility for the individual's own actions. This requires that the Mini-Society be as student-run as possible.[1]

---

[1]For a discussion of the differences in effect and affect of Mini-Societies versus Token Economies (in which imposed behavior modification is used), see M. Kourilsky and J. Hirschleifer, "Mini-Society vs. Token Economy: An experimental comparison of the effects on learning and autonomy of socially emergent and imposed behavior modification." *Journal of Educational Research,* 1976, *69*(10), 376–381.

Another pitfall is the possible stringency of the students themselves. You should emphasize that this payment activity is simply a way to get money into the system. Children can sometimes be harder on one another than an adult can be. Emphasize that the purpose of this process of selecting activities is to find ones that *all* citizens can do in order to be paid.

What types of activities and behaviors are usually selected? Some Mini-Societies have chosen to pay students for coming to school on time, for turning in assigned work on time, for obeying safety rules, etc. In one class containing a large number of physically aggressive students, Mini-Society citizens decided to be paid for not hitting anyone below the belt and for not jumping out of the windows (in a first-floor classroom, of course). The behaviors and activities students select will in large part reflect their experiences. Students often suggest payment for being "best" or "good" at something; for example, for hitting baseball homeruns, for being on the winning volleyball team, or for getting 100 percent in spelling or an A in math. You should remind students that they are trying to identify activities and behaviors that *all* have an *equal* chance of accomplishing.[2]

Once the students have decided on a few activities for which they will be paid, they must decide on amounts of payment. The amounts chosen are not important from an economic point of view. Initially, prices in the society (the degree of inflation) will scale themselves to fit the "salaries" being received. The amounts of payment chosen *are* important from the perspective of school resources. If students choose to be paid one hundred units of currency per day rather than five units per day, the time spent dittoing, cutting, and counting out the currency will increase, as will the use of paper, ditto fluid, etc. It is enticing, especially for older Mini-Society students, to choose to be paid in large amounts and therefore immediately inflate their society. It is important for you to remember that the more activities for which students choose to be paid and the higher the amounts, the less incentive there will be for the students to come up with creative business ideas. They often believe they will be richer if they award themselves larger salaries at this time. It is at times such as these that you use your elder person of state status in trying to maintain sanity without using out-and-out coercion. Payments for initial activities ideally should range from two to ten units of currency per day. This saves a great deal of confusion—and conserves the semester's paper supply. The activities for which payments will be made should be displayed on the chalkboard or on a chart so that all citizens are aware of the group decision.

2. Name Country and Currency

Early in the development of the Mini-Society approach, the name of the country and currency (as well as the flag students eventually create) seemed a secondary matter to the operation of the society and its economy. However, we have seen that Mini-Society citizens consistently take great pride in these names and symbols. Country and currency names have ranged from the mundane to the extremely inventive. Often there is a relationship between the name of the country and that of the currency, though this is not always the case. Mini-Societies have selected names such as Lollypop Land, Poohville, Land of Knowledge, Economyville, Green Acres, The United Class of Fonzies, and HaHaVille, to name a few. Currency names have ranged from poohbills, quets, and saves to millers, giggles, and rubber duckies. Students will not lack ideas for the names of their country and currency. An efficient approach for the selection of names is to have

---

[2]It is also important throughout Mini-Society that you and the students discuss those things we do for money versus those things we do as human beings. Otherwise you risk developing a situation in which the students expect to be paid for being pleasant or for saying something nice. For a more detailed discussion, see the Section titled "Should We Charge For Everything?"

students develop ideas for the names as a homework assignment rather than conducting a prolonged discussion of names in the interaction–discussion group. On the day following the homework assignment, suggested names can be listed, briefly discussed, and the matter can be settled by a quick vote.

The children may suggest naming the country and currency in your honor. You should decline gracefully if at all possible. As lovely a compliment as it may seem, a country and currency named after the teacher perpetuates the image that you control the society.

3. **Select Currency Denominations To Be Used**

In suggesting denominations for their currency, students most often name those used in the United States. Inventive students may suggest the use of odd denominations such as sevens, nines, nineteens, etc. If this situation arises, you should ask the students how they would make change in various business dealings. This is an opportune time to conduct a lesson on the arithmetic of currency denomination and change making. You may wish to assign extra-credit homework for students who attempt change-making solutions to problems presented. Bonus homework could also entail the use of the almanac or encyclopedia in which students could determine the denominations used by five or ten other countries. Sometimes without the help of this outside work a class will move directly into a discussion of change making and the value of the conventional U.S. currency system, providing themselves with a valuable math lesson. If, despite the emphasis on the convenience of a 1-5-10-20-50-100 system, the class still wishes to use other denominations (such as 17-19-21), you should not exercise veto power outright. With such an unusual currency system students will quickly become very adept at addition and subtraction. Eventually they may opt for a changeover to the more traditional denominations.

In making the final decisions on currency denominations (or on any matter being decided in the interaction–discussion group) again it is up to you to promote closure. A decision can be reached by listing all suggestions on the chalkboard and holding some form of election (show of hands or secret ballot).

4. **Select Civil Servants and the Job Criteria Each Should Meet**

The students must now decide what civil service positions they want to create, the requirements for these jobs (students may wish to use a title other than civil servant), and the rate of pay; finally they must select the persons to fill these positions. Most commonly students decide on a treasurer to be responsible for the class supply of currency and to hand out the currency on payday; several paymasters (six is usual in a class of thirty to forty) who keep track of the pay due to each student, collect the pay from the treasurer for their rows or tables, and pass out the salaries to the individuals; and expert money cutters to cut out the class currency. Often, classes will also choose to hire a permanent class recorder, although this job generally does not arise until after the first class auction. (The citizens may want jobs previously held by class monitors to be held by civil servants.)

During the discussions on appropriate qualifications for civil servants, students may wish to design applications or job forms. If you want to incorporate some career education concepts, this is a good time at which to introduce the idea of forms, interviews, and résumés. Most commonly, students will state that civil servants such as paymasters and treasurers should be good at math, have legible handwriting, not be bossy, and have a good attendance record. On one job application form designed by a group of third-graders, a space was reserved for the outline of the child's hand. I pondered for a long time the purpose therein. Perhaps this was their equivalent of taking fingerprints. However this job criterion occurred in several Mini-Societies, and when the children were asked to explain, they stated what, to them, was obvious. Because there is a great variation in physical size of class members, they wanted to be sure to select servants whose hands were large enough to handle stacks of money without dropping them. This, they explained, would save running back and forth for large amounts of money and would save having to pick up stacks of dropped bills.

In some Mini-Society classes, students decide to submit bids for performing the jobs when they submit civil service applications. Thus, if one student were willing to perform the job for less pay than other equally qualified individuals, the selection could be made on the basis of price alone. Other classes wish to set the wages of civil servants, usually paying the treasurer most and the paymasters somewhat less.

A one-time job that must be filled is that of cutting the printed currency sheets into individual bills. (Students may expect the teacher to perform this function gratis, but that won't happen.) Disputes often arise. Should their wages be based on the straightness of the cut? Should people be paid per bill cut? Should there be a reject pile for sloppy bills for which the workers are not paid? These are matters that may arise in the interaction–discussion group. In most classes three money cutters are hired as civil servants; in some classes, the problem is solved by having all citizens participate. Each would cut currency equivalent to two to four weeks of an individual's salary. Should an individual cut bills so poorly that they cannot be used, he or she would owe the treasury an equivalent amount from his or her future salary. This approach establishes the concept of the responsibility of citizen participation.

The easiest method for the selection of individuals to fill civil servant positions is to elect a committee of three to review job applications and sometimes interview the applicants. You may be asked to serve as a guiding member to ease disputes and promote closure. Upon completion of this step, the paymasters may begin to observe their designated citizens.

5. **Design the Currency and Flag for the Mini-Society, and Select the Winning Designs**
    The fifth responsibility of the students is to design both their currency faces and their flag. There are three basic methods of organization for this stage:
    - Method A—Individual students may create and submit designs for any or all currency denominations and for the flag, along with a money bid indicating how much they would charge for the production of the flag in large form and for drawing multiple renditions of the currency designs on ditto masters. The class would vote for their favorite selection.
    - Method B—Groups of students may similarly design and submit bids for currency designs and for the flag. These groups would be selected by you; students would vote for each denomination but would not be allowed to vote for the currency denomination of their own group.
    - Method C—Groups of students may be assigned to each design one denomination of the currency with an additional group designing the flag. These students would each receive a predetermined amount of compensation (money) for their work.

The students may make the determination themselves, or you may select the alternative best suited to the maturity level of the class. Method A is obviously the most realistic from an economic standpoint, B somewhat less so, and C contains almost no element of competition. It is suggested that unless your class is very immature you attempt either A or B. (Method A most closely replicates the competitive bidding for government contracts usually used in the adult world.) Method A or B allows you to introduce the concept of bidding and competition to the students before business competition within the society develops. However, the concept of competitive bidding may threaten some groups with a low degree of emotional maturity. Rather than have students immobilized by a frightening situation involving high competition, if yours is a "young" class you might do well to opt for the high degree of cooperation provided in Method C.

Before launching the design phase, you may explain to the students the function of bidding. Your introductory lesson on the function of price may include the relationship between quality and price. When making a purchase, people usually wish to pay the least amount possible, but sometimes better quality is considered a valid reason for paying a higher price. Given two items of comparable quality, people would, of course, wish to buy the one with the lower price.

In a bidding situation, the bid may or may not reflect the quality of the work. A high bid may accompany a sloppy design, although this is not always the case. Other factors may come into play. In one Mini-Society a student submitted a zero-price bid for his currency design. He was willing to work for no money if he could sign his work with a very large signature. Students decided they would rather pay someone else for drawing a currency design then to have "Pete More's" signature placed so prominently on their bills. They selected another design and paid for the artistic rendition; in this stage of Mini-Society the amount paid for the winning design comes from government. Where government obtains money will be discussed later.

Also before the designing phase, you may wish to hold a short discussion on elements of currency design. For example, a bill should probably be ornate enough to discourage counterfeiting but simple enough so that the artist can reproduce the drawn design with a good deal of consistency. The denomination and currency name should be clearly visible so that consumers and merchants alike may recognize them. If students begin to discuss varying the size and shape of the bills from the standard rectangle, you should ask them to consider wasting paper (most prevalent with a circular shape) and the ease with which bills can be cut apart from a ditto sheet. Mini-Society currency has come in a variety of shapes, such as rectangles, squares, circles, and triangles; however, the most common method of currency production has been the six equal rectangles that fill a ditto sheet. Students *may* opt for an unusual shape of currency, but try for a size and shape that fits economically on a page (such as twelve equal squares with contingent sides or equilateral triangles that can be drawn interlocking on a page).

Mini-Society currency and flag designs have ranged from cartoon characters to geometric shapes, and from dinosaurs to patriotic scenes. The students often choose to continue a theme from the country and currency name through the designs of currency and flag. Such was the case with Poohville, where the poohbills and flag were illustrated with characters from *Winnie-the-Pooh*.

6. Choose a Form of Government, If Any (Optional step)

Most of us tend to think that a government in *some* form automatically accompanies a society, but this assumption is a value judgment. It is theoretically possible to have a society with virtually no services provided or goods produced by a government. Rather than paying taxes en masse to a government to perform certain functions, individuals or groups could simply hire people to perform functions as the desires for them arise. In Mini-Society, the extent or existence of a government (this can be zero), and the form of government (should this be the chosen alternative) are decided by the students. These decisions are grave ones and should be considered carefully by the group, with your help. The students must first decide whether they wish to have a government at all.

In the interaction—discussion group, you and the students should discuss the functions of government and the fact that governments can vary greatly in type and extent of power. These general facts can be related to the Mini-Society. For example, how will the currency be run off on the ditto machine? Many schools have a regulation that only teachers can use the ditto machine. Will the students hire the teacher as a government employee or as an independent contractor to perform this function? How will the civil servants such as treasurer, paymaster, and money cutters be paid? Will students each pay some part of their own earnings directly to these workers each week, or will the civil servants be paid through some form of governmental structure (which, of course, will necessitate the eventual collection of taxes from citizens)? Most groups of students will opt for some form and amount of government out of habit and because they have come to accept government as a given; however, an introductory discussion will allow them to see that the extent of responsibility and power held by a government can vary widely, and the citizens must be willing to pay for the conveniences provided by a government. A discussion of this type will also introduce the concepts of costs and benefits of the services the students may be considering for their government.

You should also discuss with students the varying forms of government. The discussion may be quite simple or fairly complex, depending on the group of students. You may opt to use the lesson on comparative forms of government, or you may informally cover topics such as democracy versus dictatorship, pure democracy versus republic, and a presidential versus a parliamentary system.

Students may surprise you with the extent of their knowledge, although they probably will not use the standard terms for the systems they describe. Many Mini-Societies have opted for governmental systems in which the electorate choose a three- to five-person board, which then elected its own head of state from among themselves. However, they included the right to recall the head of state at any time and to have a new election at will. Students didn't know the term *parliamentary*, but that type of system is basically what they created. In promoting a decision on which (if any) form of government to have, you should remind students that they should be sure the governmental type they choose will function well within the society they hope to build and that the government can perform few or many functions but that citizens must bear the costs of these functions. Subsequent chapters contain sample lessons on government.

Once the Mini-Society citizens have accomplished their six responsibilities, the paymaster can be created, the money dittoed, and the Mini-Society formally begun.

D.   Materials Section

The following sample materials will help you get started.
1. Sample general job application form
2. Job application for treasurer
3. Job application for paymaster
4. Job application for money cutter
5. Denominations lesson: How to Build a Currency System
6. A sample letter to parents

General Job Application Form

Job Application

Name:_____

Address: _____

Date:_____

Which job do you want?_____

Why would you be good at this job?

_____

What other jobs have you had?_____

_____

Why do you want this job? _____

_____

How much do you want to get paid?

_____

Will you accept less?

☐ yes   ☐ no   ☐ maybe

sign here _____

Job Application for Treasurer

Application for Treasurer

Name:_____

Address: _____

Date applied for job:_____

Do you know what a treasurer does?
☐ yes   ☐ no

What?_____

Why will you be good at it?_____
_____

Experience:_____

MATH TEST:

$$\times\begin{array}{r}57\\8\end{array}\qquad 8\overline{)48816}\qquad \begin{array}{r}16\\17\\21\\15\\+\ 139\end{array}\qquad 37+45+8=$$

I agree that the above is true and
that I had no help on the test.

X_____

Job Application for Paymaster

Job Application for Paymaster

Name: _____

Why do you want to be Paymaster? ____

_____

Qualifications: _____

Are you honest?   ☐ YES   ☐ NO

What other jobs have you had? _____

_____

Who will recommend your work? _____

_____

What salary do you want? _____

Do this problem:

Susan did her job for 3 days at 5 rainbows a day. She also earned 2 rainbows for cleaning up. What do you pay her?

answer: _____

X _____
              signature

Job Application for Money Cutter

Application for Money Cutter

Name:_____ Date:_____

If you were money cutter and a sheet of
money fell into your desk (and no one
saw it happen) what would you do?_____

_____

_____

Why would you be good at cutting?_____

_____

List talents: 1._____ 2._____ 3._____ 4._____

Cut out these shapes and attach to
application:

Denominations Lesson: How To Build a Currency System

Good Morning, Agent #2. Because one of the functions of money is to facilitate exchange and thus make life easier, a system of money ought to be convenient. Money has to be easy to use and should make the exchange of goods and services easier.

In the past few months, we've had some odd denominations or values for our poolar bill showing up here in Poohville. Your assignment, should you decide to accept it, is to devise a system of denominations that is easy to use.

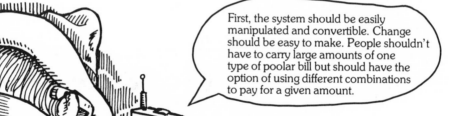

First, the system should be easily manipulated and convertible. Change should be easy to make. People shouldn't have to carry large amounts of one type of poolar bill but should have the option of using different combinations to pay for a given amount.

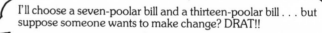

I'll choose a seven-poolar bill and a thirteen-poolar bill . . . but suppose someone wants to make change? DRAT!!

I'm terrible with numbers, but I can easily count by fives and tens. Maybe I'll make a system with five-poolar and ten-poolar bills . . .

. . . but suppose someone wanted to buy a two-poolar item? Maybe I'll add a one-poolar bill, too!

DOCUMENT

Because goods and services have arbitrary and variable prices, people must be able to generate arbitrary and variable dollar amounts out of the currency system.

- The first and simplest division: one-dollar bills.

However, one-dollar bills are impractical for individuals and businesses, because large volumes of currency must be kept around (in order to pay large amounts).

- Therefore, we need larger-valued bills. Remember that it must be easy to calculate the total value of an arbitrary collection of bills. What is easier than counting or adding by powers of ten? Next to nothing. Powers of ten are very easy to work with, because of the ease of our base-10 number system.

- Because most items in the U.S. don't cost over $100, we can use our base-10 system to make further divisions:

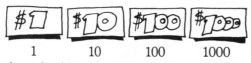

1   10   100   1000   (most obvious choices)

Watch out for this tricky question: Why not just one-dollar and hundred-dollar bills?

Simple answer: Many things cost less than $100 or between $100 and $200. You would still need a cumbersome amount of bills to make purchases or make change.

Finally, we begin to realize that lots of things cost between $10 and $100 or between $100 and $1000, etc. It seems we still have too many one-dollar bills on hand. For practicality and convenience we need some bills with in-between values. The next easiest values to work with are five and twenty. (Remember counting by fives as a kid?)

- The final currency system:

1   5   10   20   100   1000

Can you explain what went wrong in Poohville and why?

Problem:

Because Poohville only had a seven-poolar bill, all purchases or change had to be made in multiples of seven.

To make the money come out even, the person had to buy seven scoops for twenty-one poolars or pay seven poolars per scoop. Test different combinations to prove it to yourself.

The seven-poolar bill was not very convenient nor useful for making arbitrary and variable amounts of money.

A Sample Letter to Parents

Dear Parents:

  The purpose of this letter is to tell you a little about the social studies program on which we are about to embark in our classroom. We will be developing a Mini-Society, an economic education program developed by Dr. Marilyn Kourilsky, a professor at UCLA. Mini-Society is an experience-based unit, which means that economics is taught through the actual experiences of the learners. In order to create an environment where students can experience economic concepts, the students establish their own society, print their own money, open their own businesses, and live with the consequences of their own actions within the society. Your child may keep business records; write advertisements; and become a banker, newspaper writer, or insurance broker. The unit helps children understand economic concepts such as scarcity, opportunity cost, cost-benefit analysis, supply and demand, inflation, competition, and monopoly.

  In addition to the economic learnings involved in the unit there are several side benefits. The children will work actively in problem solving—trying to find creative and workable solutions to the numerous problems that occur in any society. Each student will have a voice in the decision-making process through the daily debriefings (group discussion meetings). I have found that as a result of this unit, the students are anxious to learn more about our government and how it operates both economically and legislatively.

  You can be a great help in this program by not allowing your child to take anything for Mini-Society from home without making some sort of payment. She or he can make payment through services, lazers (our money system), or allowances. An eight-dollar limit may be set for the year, although I am not advocating that you spend eight dollars on your child's class. This is the *absolute maximum* any child can spend. What we want to foster are creative ideas and entrepreneurial qualities in children. They should be encouraged to think in terms of services they can sell or things they can make for little or no money. Your active interest and involvement will enhance your child's learning.

  If enough parents want an orientation to this program, I will be happy to set up a special meeting in which I will answer any of your questions. If you are interested in such an orientation, please send a note to school with your child. In addition, you can learn much—and have a great time, too—by visiting our Mini-Society, which is in session as follows:

_____.

We welcome your visiting in accordance with our school's visiting procedure.

  Thank you for your cooperation.

                Sincerely,

E. Checklist for Chronology of Events

You will be able to determine if your Mini-Society is ready to begin procedures detailed in the next chapter by consulting this checklist. If the following items have been accomplished, it is appropriate to initiate the first infusion of currency into the economy.

After the students have adopted some sort of price system for resolving the scarcity problems, you should have helped the students to:

1. Identify behaviors for which they will be paid that
    a. are few in number ———
    b. can be accomplished by all group members ———
    c. are stated operationally ———
    d. have been posted so all are aware of the group decision ———
2. Select names for their
    a. Mini-Society country ———
    b. Mini-Society currency ———
3. Select (by vote) the currency denominations they will use in Mini-Society ———
4. Select civil service positions to be filled
    a. specifying job criteria for each position ———
    b. accepting applications for those who wish to be considered for a position ———
    c. selecting civil servants to fill the designated positions or deferring the selection until government bodies can be formed ———
5. Select a treasurer ———
6. Either individually or in groups,
    a. design possible faces for each currency denomination ———
    b. design possible flags to identify their Mini-Society ———
    c. students should determine a bid for their work if competing for winning designs ———
    d. winning designs should be selected by vote if competition is engaged in ———
7. (Optional) Discuss forms and functions of governments, and
    a. determine whether they wish to establish a formal government at this time ———
    b. if so, what form the government will take ———
    (If a government is formed and an election is required, it should be held at this point.)

CHAPTER 4

GETTING MINI-SOCIETY STARTED: THE FIRST RECEIPT OF INCOME

A.   Introduction

Approximately two to three weeks before any actual income is received in the economy, you will have introduced the initial scarcity situation, and the students will have been challenged to solve the problem of how to allocate resources when wants exceed the resources available. The following sequence of events has proved to be the most effective approach to introducing currency and diffusing the potential chaos that can result from its appearance in the economy. This format allows for minimal confusion and maximum adherence to the principles of the Mini-Society instructional system.

By following the six-step sequence you can assist the students in attaining an orderly conversion to an actual money economy. These procedures also allow for the appropriate transfer of control and power to the students themselves through the civil administrators they have hired to direct the payment activities of their societal treasury.

B.   Objectives

1. Students whose currency designs were selected for use will be able to create multiple renditions of the originals on ditto masters or in other production-ready form.
2. Upon receiving the class money supply from the teacher, the student assuming the job of treasurer will be able to supervise the cutting of currency sheets into available bills.
3. Students hired as civil servants will be able to disperse income to the citizenry according to the prespecified criteria.

C.   Six Steps for Getting the Money Supply into the System

1.   Currency Designers Create Multiple Renditions of Their Designs in Production-Ready Form

Students whose designs were selected to represent the currency denominations for the class money supply should be instructed on how to prepare their work in production-ready form. This preparation will be determined by the duplication facilities available at your school. In most schools, student designers will create multiple renditions of their designs on ditto master forms. Assuming a rectangular-shaped currency, an efficient way to duplicate the designs is to have the designer of a single denomination façade produce six renditions of the designs on one ditto master so the rectangles completely fill the page. (The renditions will be presented in two contiguous columns of three rows each, with the rows also contiguous.) To maintain some degree of consistency in the currency supply, the designers should attempt to produce the six renditions of each denomination façade so they are as identical as possible.

If your school does have facilities that allow a master to be "burned" from artwork (such as a Thermofax or Xerox machine), designers can create their multiple renditions in the same manner as previously described, but they can use a plain sheet of paper for their designs. This method is worth mentioning, because most children working on ditto master forms turn themselves into giant purple eggplant replicas. In addition, errors are more easily and clearly corrected on a plain sheet of paper than on a ditto master.

It is important to note that the creation of production-ready artwork by the currency designers is not generally considered additional work; that is, the compensation paid by the class for the design of the currency usually includes readying the design for production.

2.   The Teacher Produces the Class Money Supply on the Ditto Machine

You will produce the actual currency for the students because, in all likelihood, they will not know how to use the machine and also because school rules usually restrict the machine's use to teachers. This is an excellent time to develop the idea that your services as a teacher are not "free," because such services must be paid for by the citizens.

A rule of thumb to insure that you have created enough currency to last through one semester of Mini-Society is to go to the ditto machine and "crank 'til your arm hurts." (If the school has an automatic ditto machine, you may be understandably confused by these directions.) Another method of determining an adequate supply of currency is to multiply the number of students in the class by the amount of their maximum weekly payment for behaviors, then multiply this amount by ten. For example, 30 students × 8 (units of currency) equals 240 × 10 equals 2400. This should result in enough currency for approximately three months.

Of course, you'll want to print more of the lower denomination bills and fewer of the larger denominations for convenience in change making. Ditto masters should be put away for future use (it may be best to lock them up), because worn-out bills may have to be replaced in the course of the semester. It is also possible that the students may decide to print more money in a futile attempt to increase their society's wealth, so the masters would be required again.

One additional suggestion for the production of a class money supply is that it be done on colored ditto paper. This discourages counterfeiting and, according to some, is heartier than the white paper.

As the Mini-Society begins to function you should establish the practice of charging for your services, beginning with the insistence on compensation for creating the currency. The treasurer and paymaster are paid; shouldn't the teacher, as officer of the treasury, be paid too? As the society progresses you should decline as many functions as possible by pricing yourself out of the market—and this includes giving advice. If your consulting price is high enough, one student—or several—will enter the market to compete with you for business. You may be amazed at the number of students who stop seeking reassurance at every step and learn that they can function, at least for a while, without strict guidance from their instructor.

3. **The Teacher Transfers the Class Money Supply to the Treasurer**

Unless students have had the foresight to contract with you to use the school paper cutter for separating sheets of currency into individual bills, you should transfer the class money supply to the treasurer in its sheet form. Here may be the best time to set an example of some degree of formality in business dealings. Present the money to the treasurer with an itemized listing of what has been included; that is, indicate in writing the number of sheets printed of each denomination of currency so that there is a permanent record of the money received by the treasurer. (The treasurer may be asked to sign a receipt.) You may also wish to present a bill for services rendered in the printing of the class money supply.

4. **The Treasurer Supervises the Cutting of Currency into Individual Bills**

Provisions for cutting the money have usually been made in a prior interaction–discussion group when students made decisions concerning the hiring and functioning of civil servants. However, some brief additional discussion may arise during this step in the sequence concerning work quality and the consequences of sloppy cutting. Also, students may become concerned about others' handling of the class currency supply. Although the word *theft* may not be used, concern may be voiced that some students might pocket a few extra bills. If the concern arises, the teacher should introduce the concept of bonding—of insuring the honest action of employees hired. Bonding in a Mini-Society might be a direct function of the government or could become one of the first businesses of an enterprising young citizen. Usually at this point the children will neither be tempted to steal the newly created currency nor will they suspect others of this temptation, because most will not have internalized the future value of the currency in allowing them to purchase goods and services. If no one in the class brings up the concern, there is no need for its discussion.

5. **The Treasurer Transfers the Appropriate Amount to Each Paymaster for the First Day's Payroll**

When the paymasters have kept track of the identified behaviors for one day, they report to the treasurer income earned for their rows or tables. Of course, the paymasters should keep permanent records of these payments or transactions. The treasurer then disburses the required amount to each paymaster.

6. **The Paymasters Deliver the First Day's Wages to Their Constituents**

Having received the day's total income for their groups, the paymasters return to their rows or tables and disburse money to each student. For the first week payment should be done every day, because receiving income each day reinforces the relationship between a "job" and the income received. It also builds the trust that the Mini-Society will function as promised—that students will indeed receive income for accomplishing specific behaviors and tasks.

After three weeks of business activity, the teacher should announce to the class that the government cannot continue to produce money indefinitely and that if citizens want a continuation of government services, they must be willing to tax themselves. The payments for behaviors must also come from taxation.

Once the students know that the government will not endlessly print money to provide services and that they, the citizens, must bear the costs, their attitudes change toward the "guaranteed" annual income (a week in Mini-Society is equivalent to a year in the United States). Some classes eliminate the payments entirely. Other classes keep the payments but reduce the amounts, because, in their words, "Everyone should have a minimum income." At this juncture some teachers, depending on the grade level of their students, discuss different forms of taxation—property taxes (taxes on their desks), sales taxes on goods and services, and income taxes.

One class even decided to have a 10 percent, 20 percent, and 30 percent income tax bracket, according to an individual citizen's wealth. No class has ever autonomously come up with the idea of tax deductions.

D.   Materials Section

The following sample materials will help:
1. Samples of currency
2. Sample layouts for currency on ditto master
3. Sample flag design
4. Sample badges

Sample Layouts for Currency

Typical Currency Layout for Eight Bills to a Sheet, for Use in Mini-Society.

SAMPLE LAYOUTS FOR CURRENCY

...3 cuts (for 6 bills).

...4 cuts (for 8 bills).

...if triangles are desired.

...irregular shapes and sizes waste paper.

Sample Flag Design

Sample Badges

E.   Checklist for Chronology of Events

You can best determine if your students are ready to progress to the activities in Chapter 5 by consulting this checklist. If the following items have been accomplished, it is time to make the natural transition to a fully functioning classroom economy.

1. Have currency designers created multiple renditions of their designs in production-ready form?   ————

2. Has the teacher produced the class money supply on a duplicating machine?   ————

3. Has the teacher transferred the currency supply to the treasurer?   ————

4. Has the treasurer supervised the cutting of currency sheets into individual bills?   ————

5. Has the treasurer transferred the appropriate amount of currency to each paymaster for the first day's payroll upon

    a.   receiving each paymaster's tally of the total earnings for achievement of behaviors by her or his constituency?   ————

    b.   receiving an additional tally from paymasters of any one-time-only payments for tasks to initiate societal activity (e.g., designing currency)?   ————

6. Have paymasters delivered the first day's wages (plus one-time payments) to their constituents?   ————

Upon this first actual receipt of Mini-Society income, students are ready to begin exploring and developing the individual roles and institutional functions of an operating economy. This evolution and development is discussed in Part III, "Moving Ahead: How to Keep Mini-Society Going."

CHAPTER 5

GETTING MINI-SOCIETY STARTED—
BLOW BY BLOW: A SAMPLE SEQUENCE
OF EVENTS IN THE FIRST FIFTEEN DAYS

DAY OF MINI-SOCIETY	DAY AND WEEK	ACTIVITY
1	Monday, 1	pre-test
2	Wednesday, 1	Impose first scarcity condition; e.g., remove 5–10 desks from classroom.
3	Friday, 1	Impose second scarcity condition; e.g., ice cream certificates.

DAY OF MINI-SOCIETY	DAY AND WEEK	ACTIVITY

4	Monday, 2	• If necessary, impose other scarcity situations drawn from classroom experiences.
		
		Read scarcity fable to students (Kingdom of RumTumTum).
		
		• Debrief concept of scarcity and have students list solutions to scarcity, which include:
		
		• Put out scarcity worksheet.
		
		  ✓ first-come, first-served
		  ✓ planner (teacher) decides
		  ✓ need
		  ✓ lottery
		  ✓ auction (pay for what you want)
		  ✓ other

5	Wednesday, 2	• Challenge students to create a society that is better than the one in which they and their parents live. • Identify 3–5 activities for which they will be paid *initially*, and include amounts (display). • Send letter home to parents. • *Homework:* Think of name for country and currency.
6	Friday, 2	• Name country. • Name currency. (Put suggestions on chalkboard and let students vote.)

DAY OF MINI-SOCIETY	DAY AND WEEK	ACTIVITY
7	Monday, 3	Select denominations (math lesson).
8	Wednesday, 3	• Discuss duties of paymaster, treasurer, money cutters, and other civil servants. • Discuss tentative pay. • *Homework:* Create job application forms with job descriptions. (Give them samples.)
9	Friday, 3	• Synthesize job application forms from those submitted by students (students or teacher draw). • Choose or elect interviewers (entire class may serve as interview committee). • *Homework:* Students apply for the jobs they want.

DAY OF MINI-SOCIETY	DAY AND WEEK	ACTIVITY
10	Monday, 4	• Interview for jobs. • Select paymasters, treasurer, etc.; make final decision on pay.
11	Wednesday, 4	Create currency (one of three ways).
12	Friday, 4	• Display currency creations. • Vote for those creations the class wants. • Put currency rendition on paper to be Xeroxed or dittoed. • *Homework:* For teacher or treasurer—produce currency on Xerox or ditto machine using 10 XY rule. (Formula is $10 \cdot X \cdot Y$; Y = maximum income that could be earned by each member of the class by performing agreed-upon activities; X = number of students in class.)

DAY OF MINI-SOCIETY	DAY AND WEEK	ACTIVITY
13	Monday, 5	Create flag (one of three ways).
14	Wednesday, 5	• Display flag creations. • Vote for flag that class wants.
15	Friday, 5	• Students cut out currency. • Students give currency to treasurer or teacher. • Treasurer gives currency to paymaster. • Paymasters give currency to constituency.
16, 17		• Another payday • Exchanges
18, 19		• Another payday • Exchanges
26		• Opening of businesses • Next payday

PART III

MOVING AHEAD: HOW TO KEEP MINI-SOCIETY GOING

CHAPTER **6**

THE BEGINNINGS OF EXCHANGE

A.   Objectives

1. Within one week of receiving currency, one-quarter of the Mini-Society citizens will either buy or sell a good or service such as felt-tip pens, erasers, or tutoring services.
2. By the end of one month, every citizen in the Mini-Society will have bought and/or sold a good or service.
3. By the end of one month, at least six students (assuming an average class size of thirty) will have demonstrated entrepreneurship by opening a business in accordance with the demand of the citizens (e.g., wallet production shop, bank, etc.).
   a. In a subsequent debriefing session three characteristics of entrepreneurship will be identified by the majority of the children.
   b. At least two advantages and disadvantages of going into business for oneself versus working for others will be identified and discussed.

B.   The Spending of Income and Starting of Businesses

After the first receipt of income, your students may behave rather strangely. They will probably spend most of the Mini-Society period for a few days counting their money or looking for a place to stash it away. Some may caress the money and even kiss it. Don't worry. Most children have gotten the idea that money is a very special thing to be coveted and adored. Within a few days, however, most of them will begin to wonder what good money is if nothing can be done with it. Someone will get the idea that he or she can offer some cherished—if used—treasure to a classmate. This will start the cycle of spending that will give the students a realistic idea of what money actually is. At first the spending will take place rather casually, with children exchanging odd items from their desks or pockets for some amounts of currency. Formal business ventures will develop more slowly.

Often this first formal business is a wallet industry. After all, the students want to have a place to keep their money. Sometimes this develops as a result of a child losing her or his money in some way. Perhaps the money remains in a pocket and is washed with the clothes. Perhaps the child puts the money down somewhere and forgets it. The money may blow away on the playground or be forgotten in the card pocket of a library book. Whatever the cause, there is suddenly a demand (desire backed by the ability to pay) for wallets. Because this is the class's first formal business, it is usually swamped with customers demanding more of the good than the producer can supply. The initial price may even be raised. However, usually the following day, another child will come in with the same item (perhaps wallets, but it could be anything) and offer them for a lower price. This entry into the industry will continue as long as there is an economic profit to be made.

Students will begin to differentiate their products by designs, personalization (of the item or the service), and gimmicks. In one Mini-Society, the third wallet firm to enter the industry stole the show. Buyers were to select their wallets from a brown paper bag with their eyes closed. The reason? Some of the wallets (which were less ornate than those of competitors) had a U.S. penny in them! Note: after the first theft, a bank will usually appear on the scene.

Mini-Society businesses at first will tend to provide goods rather than services. You should try to discourage students from bringing items from home, because in so doing they do not experience out-of-pocket costs of producing an item, and some children will be at a disadvantage financially. Even if your school is quite homogeneous in income level, some children will still hold the advantage if they have parents who will go to great lengths to insure popularity and happiness by providing goods. This is an appropriate time to hold your parent orientation meeting, if you are going to have one. The meeting has distinct advantages and should be held if at all possible. First, it allows all parents an equal opportunity to ask questions. Second, it allows you to convey the enthusiasm that results from Mini-Society. When Mini-Society starts (with focusing on scarcity or with the first interaction–discussion group), begin to take random snapshots of the children at work. By the time of the parent orientation, you will have a ready-made slide show starring their own children. In tandem with your explanation of the affective and cognitive benefits of Mini-Society, this slide show can solidify the support of the parents.

During the parent orientation (and in your letter), ask for parent cooperation in limiting the goods brought from home. Ask parents to send a letter of permission with items of apparent value. This letter should state that it is all right for the item to be sold, or that the item may be used only as a capital good (that is, used for the production of other goods or services). Parents should understand that an item to be sold will not be returned; it will belong to the child who buys it. Similarly, their children will be able to keep any item they purchase. In one Mini-Society a child even brought to class a small television to auction off. When asked for a permission slip, she assured the teacher that this arrangement was perfectly OK with her parents because they had several more TVs. Needless to say, the truth had been stretched. (Another child auctioned off a hopscotch lagger for a high price. The lagger, it turned out, was her mother's 18-carat-gold necklace. It had great balance for hopscotch throwing, but the mother had other uses for it!)

A rule of thumb for importing goods from home is to set a U.S. dollar limit for each student for the entire year. Many teachers have selected a limit of eight dollars. You may wish to go lower than that, but I suggest you not go much higher. Be sure to explain that this is a *limit*—not a requirement. Students *do not* have to bring anything from home for Mini-Society. Should you have a very cooperative group of parents, you might ask them to include within this limit the value of any services they provide in the production of goods at home. A parent, for example, who helps his or her child produce chocolate-chip cookies for sale in Mini-Society should receive payment from the child in Mini-Society currency. That way parents may visit Mini-Society to spend the money and to view the system firsthand. (As a side benefit you may even get a new aide.)

Setting such a limit on goods brought from home both emphasizes out-of-pocket costs to the students and allows them to exercise greater creativity. They will have to produce goods from items available for sale at school (from your spring cleaning, the auction, or your crafts cabinet) and will also begin to think more about the types of services (low out-of-pocket costs in general) they might provide with their individual skills. Limits are reached quite quickly for some students. In one Mini-Society class, a photographer's studio was opened. Ivan charged against his limit for all the film he used and also for an assessment for the use of the camera as a capital good. However, he was quickly driven out of business by an Instant Photographer's Studio, in which another student used a 60-second camera. This second studio was swamped with business, but it didn't last long—in virtually no time the owner had used up her dollar limit on film. She then became a physical fitness coach.

What follows is a typical listing of Mini-Society businesses. Most classes develop wallet industries, banks (first as savings institutions and later for demand deposits and loans), loan services, and some services that teach crafts or physical skills. Don't be surprised if your students develop businesses quite different from those on the list. Every Mini-Society is different, reflecting the character of the group and of the individual students. Give your students free rein in developing businesses. The only limiting factors are school and district rules and the imaginations of your students.

C.   List of Businesses

1. Consulting firm (older students as well as teacher)
2. Tutorial service
3. Advertising agency
4. Clean-up service
5. Combing or hairstyling service
6. Lending library
7. Telegraph company
8. Postal service
9. Detective agency
10. Credit card company
11. Entertainment service
12. Employment agency
13. Bonding company
14. Public accounting, auditing services
15. Paramedic service
16. Learning center
17. Bank (at first savings only, but later full-service bank)
18. Loan company
19. Dance, physical fitness, and craft classes
20. Newspapers (including ads, news stories, interviews, and editorials)
21. Carpentry service
22. Wallet company
23. Artificial flower shop (flowers sold singly or in arrangements)
24. Snack bar
25. Junk shop
26. Boutique
27. Race track (either providing time trials for owner-provided cars or with provisions for betting on winning cars)
28. Souvenir shop (especially if many visitors come to Mini-Society or if you participate in international trade with other classes)
29. Lottery game
30. Bankers for international trade (buyer and seller of money)

31. Printing shop (providing business cards, letterhead paper, etc.)
32. Make-your-own shop (in which consumers pay to use materials and supplies in the creation of, for example, painted-rock paperweights)
33. Legal services (including judges for hire in civil suits)
34. Window dressing service (to set up business displays)

D.   The Roles of the Teacher and Principal

As business exchange in Mini-Society begins and the economy becomes operational, a reminder of the teacher's role as well as that of the principal seems desirable. After the first receipt of income, your participation in Mini-Society becomes less visible. Specifically, your role becomes that of citizen, consultant, facilitator, and businessperson.

As a citizen, you have had more experience than any other member of the society and should therefore share your wisdom with the other citizens. However, remember that you are only one citizen, and your well-meant advice may be rejected.

You may also use the Mini-Society period to give advice as a paid consultant. Although many children believe that you were born in the classroom and have never ventured beyond it, they soon learn you are a valuable resource, and they'll seek advice on such matters as colors to use in logos, how much to charge for a product, or even whether to work for themselves or someone else.

Your basic role as facilitator depends upon your acute observations of activities in the classroom. As you observe experiences in Mini-Society you will be selecting those issues with economic, political, and legal content, and those which require values clarification, to debrief with the group. After business activities for the day have been concluded you will organize the class into their interaction—discussion groups to define and analyze these experiences. It is through these debriefing sessions that students cement their learning of basic concepts and ideas. A specific format for debriefing and a sample debriefing lesson will be included in Part IV of this book.

In the early stages of Mini-Society you will probably be debriefing each day for ten to fifteen minutes. This time is included in the thirty-five to sixty minutes of Mini-Society for which you have planned. Later, you may be debriefing as little as once a week, depending on current activities. Students occasionally may wish to spend an entire Mini-Society period on a particular debriefing. They also may wish to hire a consultant (from inside or outside the school) to instruct the entire group in a particular business method or concept. (For example, some groups hire a local banker to give them information on how banks make profits.)

Nothing prevents you, the teacher, from going into business for yourself and displaying your entrepreneurial skills. Two of our local teachers, in fact, discovered they were so entrepreneurially oriented that they left teaching and went into business! Both were quite successful and reported that most of what they had learned about business was in the course of being a Mini-Society teacher.

The school principal starts out in Mini-Society as a land baron of sorts. Because the students initially own only their desks and the immediate surrounding area, they often rent space from their neighbors in order to conduct business. However, if they wish to use the halls, auditorium, or playground for business activity, they must negotiate a deal with the principal. One very enterprising student went into the principal's office about the third week of Mini-Society and offered to buy out all her interests for five hundred fonzies (the students' unit of currency). Later, when the principal visited the class to buy some birthday cards, she discovered what a poor deal she had made and insisted she had been taken. She demanded to exchange the five hundred fonzies in return for her real estate. The class in a debriefing session decided that a deal was a deal, and they hoped that next time the principal would know better.

E.   Measuring Mini-Society Progress

What if your Mini-Society is slow to develop businesses? How will you know if progress is satisfactory? The following two economic indicators can be used to judge the progress of your class. They are not economic indicators in the same sense as are the GNP, NNP, or the Consumer Price Index. They are guidelines or signposts, developed after years of Mini-Society observation and testing, and they measure progress in relationship to previous Mini-Societies.

1. *Economic Progress Indicator I.* Within *one week* after receiving the first income (assuming you conduct Mini-Society for one period, three days a week), one-fourth of the Mini-Society citizens should be buying and/or selling goods and services. These exchanges do not have to be of a formal nature; they may be the first casual exchanges mentioned earlier.

2. *Economic Progress Indicator II.* Within *one month* (ten to twelve Mini-Society days) of the first receipt of income, at least one-sixth of the students should have demonstrated enterpreneurship by opening businesses in accordance with citizens' demands. This indicator refers to the more formal business venture. To be in accordance with the demand of the citizens means that the entrepreneur has attempted to sell a good or service that at least some of the citizens want and are willing to pay for.

A class may not meet these indicators on schedule for a number of reasons. (1) Some teachers are not able to conduct Mini-Society for the recommended period of time each week (three times a week for forty-five minutes each day), which naturally slows down the progress. (2) Some classes may be slower to trust the system. You have explained that in Mini-Society the students will not receive penalties from you for any actions that do not break school or safety rules, but they may be slow to believe you. They may be waiting for some cue for the actions expected of them. Mini-Society may seem like too much fun to be real. (3) Many students have never had much responsibility before. They may be frightened of even buying one item for fear of making a "bad" decision. (4) Students may simply not know where to begin.

A more unusual reason for slow progress may be a low level of trust among the students themselves. In one fourth grade class, only a very few businesses had opened after a month. The students talked of opening a bank but one somehow never got started. They asked the teacher to be banker. She refused, but said she would consult with the banker to help set up the business. Still, no bank appeared. She finally discovered that no two students trusted a third to hold their money. This is a sad commentary but reflects the attitudes that may be brought to a Mini-Society from the outside world. It must be remembered that the neighborhood environments of the children will differ greatly across the U.S. and that Mini-Societies will show great variation.

What can be done if the Mini-Society is not progressing satisfactorily? A lack of trust within the group can be dealt with through values clarification lessons held in the interaction–discussion group; only time and effort will produce a solution. If your problem is students who are fearful of making decisions, reinforce them whenever they make any decisions—no matter how bad. This problem is usually one that affects just a few children, not the whole class, so it shouldn't paralyze the society to any extent.

To cope with any of these problems, but especially with the most common one of students not knowing where to begin, the teacher may facilitate business activity in the following ways: (1) establish a learning center on how to start a business; (2) establish a class auction; (3) have each student list at least one idea for a business venture; and (4) hire consultants, including older children, parents, and yourself. Regardless of how well business activity is progressing, I would suggest that *all teachers* implement the strategies of establishing a learning center, and a class auction, to be discussed in the next two chapters.

CHAPTER 7

HOW TO START A BUSINESS

A.   Objectives

After completing the activities in this chapter, students will be able to:

1. Generate at least one idea for a business venture (by the end of two months of Mini-Society activity), in accordance with the demand of Mini-Society citizens.
2. Conduct a market survey to assess the demand of the other Mini-Society citizens.
3. Convert a market survey to a demand curve.
4. State verbally or in writing two factors that should be considered before choosing a business location.
5. List three types of costs associated with starting a business.
6. Explain why rent is a cost of production.
7. List three ways of obtaining money to start a business.
8. Draw two types of advertising appeals.
9. Keep business records accurately by (a) listing all business expenses; (b) listing all sales; and (c) determining the resulting profit or loss.

Sometimes the students have ideas for businesses but simply do not know where to begin, or they are afraid to take that first step into the unknown. Many major economic and governmental concepts will be passed on to the students in debriefings in the latter weeks of a Mini-Society semester. These discussions are outlined for you in detail in Chapters 9 to 13. Students may launch into their businesses, however, after only a few basic ideas have been presented and reinforced.

We have already reviewed both the logistics and the progressive structuring of events in the development of Mini-Society. As children begin to explore entrepreneurial possibilities, you may need to provide them with a solid foundation of business concepts. This chapter explores six areas of economic expertise upon which you may draw during these initial stages and outlines some simple methods for dispensing this added background and insight.

You can help make business a more understandable and comfortable concept by providing simple learning centers, games, bulletin boards, and discussions to introduce and reinforce business concepts. Some of the aspects that should be covered include:

1. Assessing the demand for products, including assessing the characteristics of possible competing products.
2. Choosing a business location and obtaining any required license.
3. Determining costs of materials, labor, etc.
4. Obtaining money to start the business, including alternatives such as taking

out a loan, selling stock, or using personal resources.
5. Recording and keeping business records.
6. Advertising the business—how and why—along with other aspects of business expansion and marketing techniques.

If students have already covered many of the topics through the dilemmas, then one learning center could be used to review all the steps. A key listing each of the concepts to be reinforced may be prepared, accompanied by instructional topic folders that outline each concept in detail.

Example:

If students have not covered these concepts through dilemmas or discussion, a general overview may not provide enough information. If this is the case, individual learning centers may be employed covering each of the topics in detail. Following are some suggested activities that might be used as students prepare to start their businesses. While many of these concepts may come naturally to some children, others will need the added input that learning centers and instructional practice sheets can offer.

B.   Assessing Demand

You will be teaching students to conduct a market survey to assess the demand for their possible products or services. Before they do a survey, the students must have an introduction to the factors determining demand. They will need to become familiar with methods of evaluating the demand for products, including assessing the characteristics of possible competing products. Your learning center for demand might include the following components.

1.   Conduct a Market Survey

(a)   Ask twenty students whether they prefer to eat bananas or grapes. Record results on a worksheet (#1), using tally marks.

Bananas	Grapes
JHT	JHT
IIII	JHT II

(b)   Of the fruit they preferred (the majority), record how many they would buy at the following prices. Record on a worksheet (#2).

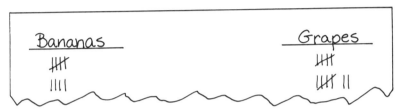

How many (grapes) would you buy if they each cost:
$1.00   (0)
  .75   (III)
  .50   (JHT II)
  .25   (JHT JHT JHT JHT)
  .05   (JHT JHT JHT JHT JHT JHT)

The next section of the learning center would focus on recording the market survey information on a demand schedule and drawing a demand curve.

2.   Record Results on a Demand Schedule

Fill in the information from your market survey on worksheets. List the total quantity (of grapes) demanded for each price:

Demand Schedule Worksheet

Price	Quantity
$ 1.00	(0)
.75	(3)
.50	(7)
.25	(20)
.05	(30)

3.   Draw a Demand Curve

The information from the demand schedule can also be shown by drawing a demand curve. A third section of this learning center might illustrate this procedure in simple, sequential steps:

(a) On a piece of graph paper, draw two lines (one vertical and one horizontal).

(b) Label the vertical line "P" for price and the horizontal "Q" for quantity.

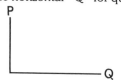

(c) Starting with zero (where the P and Q come together), section off squares on the graph paper, and label the prices and quantities used on the demand schedule.

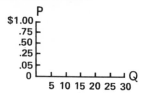

(d) Record the information from the demand schedule, using dots at the point where the price intersects with the quantity.

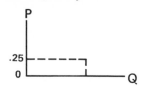

(e) After all the dots have been placed, draw a curve or a continuous line to connect them.

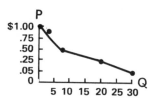

If your class needs help in following the procedure the first time around, you may want to walk it through with them as a group. A learning center that includes all the concepts of demand and supply as illustrated might look something like this:

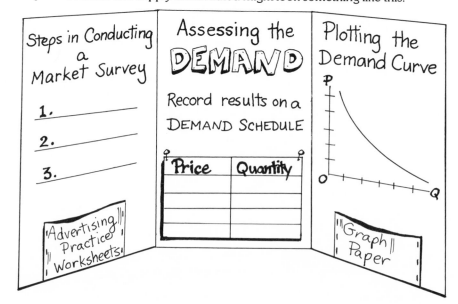

An additional way for students to determine if others will buy their product is to look at the complements and substitutes within their classroom. (Complements are products that go with other products. Substitutes are products used in place of other products.) For example, if Chris has a thriving movie threater, will Kathy be better off selling popcorn (complement) or opening a puppet theater (substitute)? If Terri's weaving shop is doing very poorly, will Tricia be better off opening up a yarn store (complement) or another kind of craft shop (substitute)?

Worksheets may be included in the learning center for students to list complements and substitutes for a particular product. For example:

List three complements and three substitutes for chocolate chip cookies:

Complements	Substitutes
1. _____	1. _____
2. _____	2. _____
3. _____	3. _____

OR:

List one substitute for the following products:

beef _____

lemonade _____

movie _____

lettuce _____

List one complement for the following products:

pencils _____

tennis rackets _____

records _____

eggs _____

Those of you teaching in the lower grades may wish to provide games in which students receive practice in matching complements and substitutes. One of these games is to cut circles out of poster board and glue or draw a picture of a product on one half of the circle and a picture of its complement or substitute on the other half of the circle. When the circle is cut in half and a number of semicircles are mixed together, the students will match the two that go together (forming the complete puzzle). Ask students to tell whether it is a complement or a substitute, and write the answer on the back so that they can check themselves.

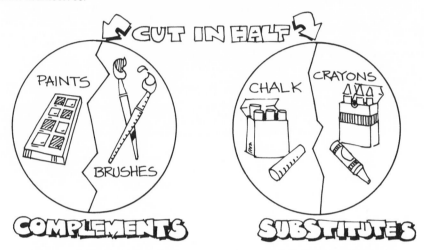

Another game is to have separate cards with pictures of products and the complements of those products along with pictures of products and the substitutes of those products. The students will put a "C" clothespin on the two that go together as complements or an "S" clothespin on the two that are substitutes for each other.

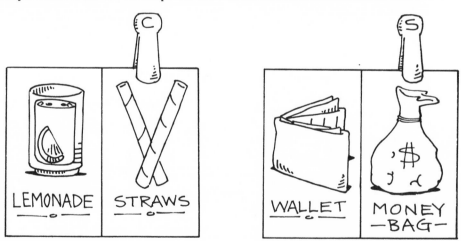

C.   Choosing a Location

Information in your learning center on choosing a business location and obtaining a business license must be tailored to your own Mini-Society. In general, the determination of business location requires that the young entrepreneurs consider which locations are available and weigh the quality of the locations against the various rental fees for these. In Mini-Society you can discuss classroom traffic patterns, indicating that a business located in a busy traffic route may be more successful due to high visibility and easy access. There is almost always heavy traffic in an elementary school classroom near the pencil sharpener, the teacher's desk, the cloak room doors, and the drinking fountain. Of course, rental fees may be higher for these locations.

Another consideration in deciding where to locate a Mini-Society business concerns a mid-room location versus one along the wall or chalkboard. These latter locations have the obvious advantage of providing a place for business signs (and possible displays); also, spaces along the chalkboard have the built-in advantage of use of that section of the board. Mid-room locations may present serious problems: How will business signs be made to stand up? Can buyers easily get to and from these stores? In some Mini-Society classes, citizens will decide that they will automatically hold ownership of their desks, so they will then be free to use these for their own business locations or to rent them to others. (In such a case students will probably come up with some type of lease agreement.) In other classes, students will decide that any citizen may rent any desk space for use as a Mini-Society business; a particular space will go to the highest bidder, who pays rent to the class treasury. Some classes choose to supplement the treasury by collecting an additional fee from business owners—the business license fee. (This fee also curbs the temptation to try going into a new business every other day.)

If your class has exercised this latter option, be sure to outline steps for obtaining such a license in your learning center. The learning center should not only explain to the students why business licenses are sometimes required and how to obtain one in your particular classroom but should also afford them an opportunity to practice filling out any necessary forms. The following is a sample lease agreement and business license that might be used in your learning center, along with specific instructions.

Lease Agreement

_____ SCHOOL

NAME _____ BUSINESS _____

LOCATION _____

I, _____, of _____ business,

do hereby agree to pay the amount of _____ every _____ days, for use

of the desks, tables, etc., that I may be renting from the city.

I agree to pay this amount to the treasurer, _____.

Signature _____

Business License

Name of owner(s) _____

Type of business _____ Name of business _____

Location _____

I hereby promise I will conduct business in an orderly fashion and according to

the laws established by _____ Mini-Society.

Signature _____
owner(s)

Signature _____
class official

THIS BUSINESS LICENSE MUST BE ON DISPLAY
DURING BUSINESS HOURS

D.   Determining Expenses

You will also want your learning center to include information on determining the necessary operating costs of a business. Although each potential business will have different specific operating costs, your goal here will be to make the students more aware of out-of-pocket costs in general. Because you won't be able to anticipate all the particular costs for each student, introduce them to broad categories of these expenses. You will probably wish to give examples of their initial costs such as desk rent, business license fee, salaries, advertising expenses, costs of raw materials, repayment of loans, rent on any equipment, consultant fees, etc. Be sure that students understand a basic goal of business owners: to cover out-of-pocket costs and have additional money left over in the form of profit. You can provide some worksheets that allow the students to practice figuring expenses for some hypothetical Mini-Society businesses. The following are examples.

Julie's Jewelry Store

During a two-week period, Julie's expenses included:

materials	40 C's
rent	5
employee salaries	10
consultant fee	2
TOTAL EXPENSES	_____

Julie's Jewelry Store made the following sales:

Monday	10 C's
Wednesday	12
Friday	10
Monday	7
Wednesday	13
Friday	10
TOTAL SALES	_____

Did Julie's Jewelry Store make a profit or a loss _____? How much? _____

Many students won't know exactly how much to charge for their products in order to cover expenses and to allow for a profit. If they charge too much, they may price themselves out of business. You can instruct them in the learning center on how to make a supply schedule and establish the equilibrium price (the point at which quantity demanded equals quantity supplied). The design of this learning center may be very similar to the demand/supply center. Again, instruction should be clear and in small steps that are self-checking.

SUPPLY SCHEDULE

Record the following amounts of your product that you are willing to supply at the various prices listed:

Supply Schedule	
Price	Quantity
1.00	20
.75	15
.50	13
.25	6
.05	0

This information can also be shown by drawing a supply curve on a graph as you did with the demand schedule by drawing a demand curve.

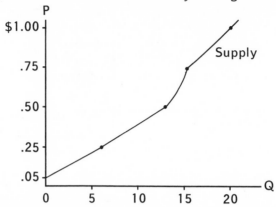

When both curves are drawn, you can see *Equilibrium Price*, which is the intersecting point at which the quantity demanded equals the quantity supplied.

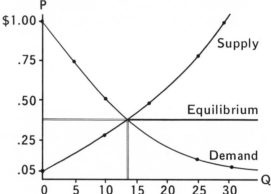

E.   Obtaining Capital

In discussing various methods of obtaining capital to start a business, you'll want to present the specifics of each method along with a discussion of its advantages and disadvantages. For example, the use of personal savings as starting capital means that the business owner has no monthly repayments to make and must pay no interest on a loan. However, it may take quite a long time to save enough money, and meanwhile someone else may get the same idea. Another disadvantage of using personal savings is the opportunity cost in terms of the personal consumables that would have to be foregone. In examining the possibility of a business loan from a bank or loan company, be sure your students understand that the lender will charge interest for the use of her or his money.

Discuss possibilities that may exist within your own Mini-Society: Is there a bank or loan company that might be willing to make the loan? Is there an individual with enough money to make such a loan? At what interest rate? When must the loan be repaid? Discuss procedures for taking out a loan, including the skills needed for filling out the necessary forms and the possible interview with the lender. A bank, loan company, or even an individual will probably require some indication that the borrower will be able to repay the money on time. The lender may wish some details about the potential business to see if it will be a good risk and in some cases may ask for some form of collateral. Following is a sample bank loan application that might be used in familiarizing students with the process of obtaining cash.

```
┌─────────────────────────────────────────────────────────────────────────┐
│                        Bank Loan Application                              │
│                                                                           │
│  NAME _____  GRADE _____          │
│                                                                           │
│  CLASSROOM _____  DATE _____           │
│                                                                           │
│  JOB(S) _____          │
│                                                                           │
│  WEEKLY INCOME _____  AMOUNT OF LOAN _____          │
│                                                                           │
│  REASON FOR LOAN _____            │
│                                                                           │
│  AMOUNT OF INTEREST _____                                       │
│                                                                           │
│  AMOUNT TO BE PAID BACK IN FULL BY _____            │
│                                                                           │
│  REFERENCES _____                            │
│                                                                           │
│              _____                          │
│                                                                           │
│              _____                 │
│              Signature                                                    │
│                                                                           │
│              _____                 │
│              Banker's Signature                                           │
└─────────────────────────────────────────────────────────────────────────┘
```

Besides giving the students experience in filling out forms such as these, your learning center might include skills lessons in figuring interest rates, the net amount to be paid, and the frequency and amount of individual payments.

Some of these same principles apply to selling stock in the company. In discussing stock sales with your students, avoid being too complex. Unless they have a seat waiting for them on the New York Stock Exchange or are quite sophisticated in financial matters, you will not need to go into detail such as the differences between common and preferred stock. Rather, you can simply explain that selling a share of stock means that an owner is selling a small portion of his or her business to the investor. Some entrepreneurs who find it difficult to obtain loans or are uncomfortable owing money resolve this conflict by selling stock in their business enterprises. The stockholder provides some money for the business operation and in return receives a certificate indicating how much of the business she or he owns. Stockholders, like banks, usually want some indication that the business is a good risk for them. They want to invest in a business that has a good chance of making a profit, because, traditionally, they receive dividends— some portion of the profit—at intervals. You might mention that it is wise for an owner to sell only a part of the business through stock transactions. The owner will probably want to retain at least 51 percent of the shares in the business if he or she wants to continue running and controlling it.

F.   Record Keeping

Many Mini-Society citizens fail in business because they have no idea (or inclination) of how to keep business records. Stan reported gleefully to his teacher that he had made 200 schayas (their currency) on his custom-made kites. He was really excited until his teacher asked him how much it had cost him to make the kites. When Stan realized his expenses had been 331 schayas (and that he had only taken in 200 schayas in sales), he became less ecstatic. He requested on his own behalf and in the interest of others who shared similar experiences that the teacher provide a lesson on record keeping. The following are some examples of worksheets you may wish to use to reinforce the importance of record keeping.

Expense Ledger

Current Date: _____   Posted Date: _____

Name of Business: _____

EXPENSES:

Wages: _____ $ _____

                _____   _____

Rent: _____   _____

                _____   _____

Materials: _____   _____

                _____   _____

                _____   _____

                _____   _____

                _____   _____

Other: _____   _____
(list)

                _____   _____

                _____   _____

                        TOTAL EXPENSES: $ _____

Money Received

Date _____

Items: Amount:

_____ $ _____

_____   _____

_____   _____

_____   _____

_____   _____

_____   _____

_____   _____

_____   _____

_____   _____

_____   _____

                          TOTAL: $ _____

Business Record-Keeping Sheet

Name of Business: _____

Owners' Names: _____

_____

_____

Date: _____			Date: _____		
Month	Day	Year	Month	Day	Year
Money received:		$_____	Money received:		$_____
Less expenses:		$_____	Less expenses:		$_____
Equals			Equals		
Total profit:		$_____	Total profit:		$_____
Or total loss:		$_____	Or total loss:		$_____
Date: _____			Date: _____		
Month	Day	Year	Month	Day	Year
Money received:		$_____	Money received:		$_____
Less expenses:		$_____	Less expenses:		$_____
Equals			Equals		
Total profit:		$_____	Total profit:		$_____
Or total loss:		$_____	Or total loss:		$_____
Date: _____			Date: _____		
Month	Day	Year	Month	Day	Year
Money received:		$_____	Money received:		$_____
Less expenses:		$_____	Less expenses:		$_____
Equals			Equals		
Total profit:		$_____	Total profit:		$_____
Or total loss:		$_____	Or total loss:		$_____

Sample Lesson

Each of these companies kept careful records. Their income and expenses are listed below. Write the word *profit* or *loss* in each box, depending upon how well the business did.

Raincoat Company	Canoe Company
Sales $200	Sales $250
Rent $40	Rent $100
Labor $50	Labor $75
Materials $100	Materials $125

Fishing Pole Company	Boot Company
Sales $178	Sales $635
Rent $30	Rent $175
Labor $40	Labor $200
Materials $105	Materials $300

Sleeping Bag Company	Goggles Company
Sales $149	Sales $298
Rent $50	Rent $46
Labor $50	Labor $51
Materials $50	Materials $200

Extra Challenge:

Which company made the most profit? _____

Which company suffered the worst loss? _____

G.   Advertising and Business Expansion

As new businesses are born and competition arises, students will naturally become aware of the possibility of selling their products through advertising. In discussing the how and why of advertising, you are dealing with the concepts of consumer sovereignty and demand. Businesses advertise because, in the long run, consumer spending will decide which products remain on the market and which do not. Their success or failure depends on pleasing customers. Advertising is an attempt to get consumers to buy one product instead of another, and it involves a number of complex factors. An advertisement must attempt to differentiate the product from other products in the minds of the consumers. You may wish to include in your learning center pictures and advertisements of the same product (such as soap, dog food, toothpaste), but with each advertisement showing how one company's product differs from the others. The purpose of advertising is to make consumers willing to buy a larger quantity of the product at a whole range of prices (not just the current price). In economics we refer to this as a change (or increase) in demand.

When discussing advertising with your students, you might cover different types of appeals used in ads (such as the bandwagon appeal or the testimonial approach) and discuss these different methods and their purposes and effectiveness. Advertisements illustrating the various methods and appeals could be included in the center, and the student would be asked to identify which appeal is being used in each advertisement.

You may want to use some of the following appeals and methods:
Bandwagon—"everyone" is buying the product.
Comparison—shows that one product is better than another.
Security—use of product will make you feel safe.
Testimonial—someone explains how effective she or he feels a product is.
Celebrity testimonial—famous person endorses product.
Health—use of product will improve your health.

Students could also be asked to describe and illustrate three ways of advertising a product using various appeals and methods. These ads could then be displayed on a bulletin board. If this concept has already arisen in your Mini-Society, you may wish to cover truth-in-advertising concepts in your learning center.

Following is an example of a learning center that reinforces many of these concepts. It includes examples of advertising methods and gives practice in identifying and generating advertisements of various types.

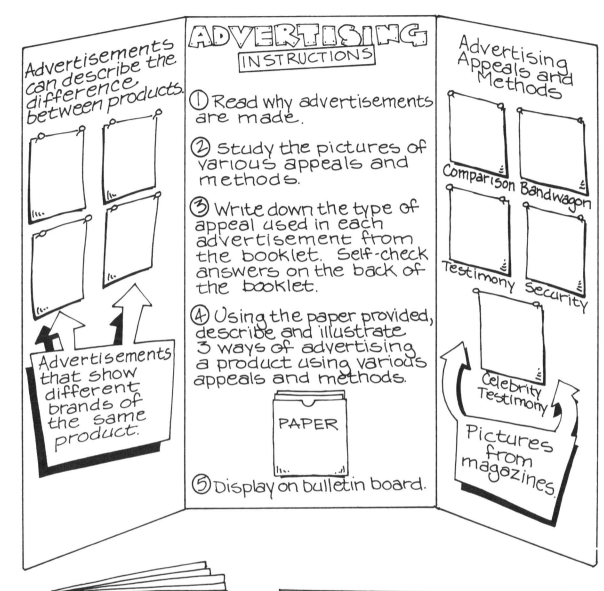

Advertisements can describe the difference between products.

Advertisements that show different brands of the same product.

ADVERTISING
INSTRUCTIONS

① Read why advertisements are made.

② Study the pictures of various appeals and methods.

③ Write down the type of appeal used in each advertisement from the booklet. Self-check answers on the back of the booklet.

④ Using the paper provided, describe and illustrate 3 ways of advertising a product using various appeals and methods.

PAPER

⑤ Display on bulletin board.

Advertising Appeals and Methods

Comparison   Bandwagon

Testimony   Security

Celebrity Testimony

Pictures from magazines.

ADVERTISING Appeals and Methods Booklet

Advertisements that students will identify according to the particular appeal or method used. (Answers on back of booklet.)

In at least a rudimentary fashion, you now know the steps in starting a business. Of course, the most important ingredient of a successful business is a good idea; however, many people have the ideas but do not know where to begin. They need help in orchestrating their ideas so that their originality eventually becomes manifested in a thriving business. This chapter has attempted to provide you with ideas, suggestions, and worksheets for showing even young children how to go about starting a business within their Mini-Society. These skills may be transferrable to our larger society, and, as a result of your instruction, many more individuals may have the option of working for themselves rather than working for someone else.

CHAPTER **8**

THE AUCTION AND OTHER METHODS FOR FACILITATING BUSINESS ACTIVITY

A.   Objectives

After completing the activities in this chapter, students will:

1. Be able to identify the main elements of an auction and decide to participate as buyers, sellers, auctioneers, and/or observers, listing the advantages and disadvantages of each role.
2. Volunteer to play the role of auctioneer and show competency in the following areas (at least one student will do this):
    (a) soliciting the items to be auctioned
    (b) soliciting minimum buying prices from the potential sellers
    (c) ascertaining whether the potential sellers want to auction the items themselves or pay a fee or percentage to the auctioneer
    (d) providing for the recording of buyer, seller, and purchase price for each item auctioned[1]
    (e) conducting the auction and demonstrating verbal skills, including sufficient voice volume, articulation, and variation; and recognizing all potential bidders
3. Participate in the auction by making a bid and/or buying an item (at least one-third of the students will do this).
4. Be able to describe the role and importance of a business consultant.

B.   The Auction and its Benefits

The auction is a source of much excitement as well as a strategy for increasing business activity. Most classes enjoy it so much that it becomes a weekly Mini-Society institution. In addition to stimulating entrepreneurial ventures, the auction offers the following benefits:

1. Students are motivated to participate as earners in their Mini-Society in order to be able to purchase goods and services at the auction.
2. Students discover that they can receive higher prices for their products when their market is larger and buyers are bidding against each other.
3. Students discover what is demanded by other Mini-Society citizens, and the subsequent buying and selling of goods and services increases, reflecting their new knowledge of the marketplace.

---

[1]This function is often performed by a civil servant.

4. The heightened activity in the marketplace increases the circulation of money in the economy—it "primes the pump."

5. Verbal skills are enhanced, because students must describe their items and articulate the characteristics of what they are trying to sell. Math skills and record-keeping skills can also be increased as a result of auction activity.

A few hints regarding the operation of an auction can mean the difference between organization and chaos. Record keeping is essential. As in the adult world, many conflicting claims arise from verbal agreements. Merchandise to be offered should be received before the auction begins. Last-minute additions offered in the frenzied atmosphere of bidding can make the auction a nonstop, all day affair. No more than five pupils should be allowed to sign up at one time to auction a product. One item per pupil may be auctioned. Each time the class has an auction a different allocation mechanism should be employed to determine who goes first, second, third, fourth, and fifth. For example, on a given day positions in the auction can be determined on a first-come, first-served basis. On another day the auctioneers can have a lottery to determine their position in the auction. Other options include the teacher deciding, the auctioneers bidding for their positions, and force.[2] The advantages and disadvantages of these alternative distribution mechanisms can be discussed later in the debriefing sessions so that the students will have more and more experience in determining the way in which they believe rewards or output should be distributed in an economy.

It is recommended that students only auction items that have been produced in their classroom societies. However, if they wish to bring items from home, you may permit them so long as they bring only the *resources*, or raw materials, and not final products from home. They must combine these resources within the classroom to create their final product. Also, any items from home should be counted in the eight-dollar maximum[3] they are allowed to utilize from sources outside the classroom. If items from home are allowed, you should write a letter to the parents explaining the auction and its purpose. You should also scan the list of merchandise to be sure that items that seem to have substantial monetary or sentimental value have not been brought from home without parental (or sibling) permission. In developing your Mini-Society auction, be sure to consider the steps for organizing the auction, procedures for conducting an auction, and suggestions for keeping records.

C.   Three Steps for Organizing an Auction

1. *Solicit items to be auctioned.* This should be done several days ahead of the auction, soliciting approximately five items. Post a sign-up sheet for this purpose.

2. *Establish a minimum price for each item to be auctioned.* This information should be provided on the sign-up sheet by the sellers. This process saves time, because without a minimum bid each item would probably start at one unit of currency and work its way up, and it also saves tears. Students may be offering items they would not wish to sell for less than a certain minimum.

3. *Ascertain if an auctioneer is to be hired.* This information also should be indicated on the sign-up sheet by the sellers. Some sellers feel confident in their own ability to generate a high price, or they may not wish to share their profit (or loss) with an auctioneer. In that case they will auction the item themselves. Some children, at least in the beginning, are too shy to get up and sell an item in front of the whole class.[4]

[2]They can have an arm-wrestling contest.
[3]Some classes may have less than an eight-dollar maximum, and others may allow absolutely no items from home.
[4]Some third graders are so small they will only volunteer to auction if they are allowed to stand on a chair.

You probably will have some highly verbal—and "hammy"—children who wish to hire out their auctioneering services, especially after the first auctions. These auctioneers may charge a flat fee or some percentage of the total sales price.

D.   Four Steps Necessary for Conducting an Auction

1. ***Auctioneer describes item and tells minimum bid.*** The item should be held in plain view. Some classes have experimented with a preview period in which the items can be viewed up close. This works well for most classes. In a few other instances, though, the disputes over breakage have proved prohibitive.

    Before or during the first auction, you may feel it necessary to demonstrate auctioneering technique. Do this only if the children are very reticent to try themselves. Do not become the class auctioneer—it is simply another element of control that you and your students can do without; simply price your auctioneering services out of the market.

2. ***Students raise hands to bid and state their offer when called on; or they hold up bid cards when a price they are willing to pay is called.*** The method you choose will be largely controlled by two factors: your own noise-tolerance level and your relationship with neighboring teachers. The method using spoken bids often becomes quite noisy, with children enthusiastically yelling out before they are called on; however, most children prefer this method to using bid cards. With a highly volatile or a highly sophisticated group, the idea of bidder cards should be introduced occasionally if for no other reason than to provide variety. Each person wishing to bid receives a numbered card. There is no vocal bidding. Cards are raised in response to the auctioneer's patter. ("Who'll give me twenty? Number Seven bids twenty. Who'll give me thirty? twenty-five? Number Five bids twenty five. Who'll give me thirty? Going once, twice, sold for twenty-five to Number Five.") Obviously, this method provides a quiet, controlled situation where needed and is useful if the auction is taking place while business is being conducted in the same room.

3. ***Winning bidder pays civil servant for the item.*** A civil servant should be hired to exchange the bought item for the currency owed and to deliver the money to the item's seller. The seller is responsible for paying her or his own auctioneer, if she or he has hired one. This allows the auction to continue while the transactions are finalized.

4. ***Civil servant records data: name of buyer, name of seller, auctioneer, amount of final bid, item, and date of purchase.*** This record keeping serves several functions. It reinforces the concept that records should be kept in any business venture, it provides information should a later dispute arise over payment, and it also comprises an interesting tool for use in debriefing throughout the semester. Students can chart the differences in prices of items between auctions and regular business. Having this record of what items were in demand, they get an idea of prices paid for various items and can chart inflationary and recessionary trends in their society.

E.   Suggestions for Keeping Records

Sign-Up for the Auction

	Name of Seller	Name of Auctioneer (if not same)	Item to be Auctioned	Minimum Bid	Date of Auction
1.					
2.					
3.					
4.					
5.					

Record of the Auction

	Name of Buyer	Name of Seller	Auctioneer	Item Auctioned	Amount of Final Price	Date of Purchase
1.						
2.						
3.						
4.						
5.						

F.   After the Auction

Several rules of conduct are connected with a Mini-Society auction. Of course, the usual safety and courtesy rules apply, but, further, there is an economic rule. Winning bidders *must pay* the amount they bid on items, even if they have to borrow to do this. The first time this happens in a class, a loan shark usually appears, which may or may not be the first instance of a money-lending business in the Mini-Society. However, the rates charged for money loaned at auctions are almost always usurious. This has been very simply explained by past Mini-Society citizens with, "If they're careless enough to bid more than they have, they deserve to pay high interest rates."

After an auction, the teacher may wish to assemble the class into an interaction–discussion group to debrief some of the events of the auction. Such questions as the following are relevent:

1. Why do you think Sally decided to sell her product at auction instead of at her store?
2. Do you think Sally could have received a higher or lower price for her product if she had sold it at her store instead of at the auction?
3. What was the effect of students bidding against each other? Did the bidding raise or lower the price received for Sally's product? Do you think the process of bidding against each other is fair?
4. What are the advantages and disadvantages of an auction—to the seller and to the buyer?

5. What is the difference between describing your product "to its fullest extent" and misleading the consumers? Can you relate this difference to truth in advertising?

6. Can you think of any reasons why your parents might wish to be buyers or sellers in an auction?

Many teachers have asked, "How do you end the Mini-Society experience? Do you just walk into a class one day and say this is it?" We have found that a final auction is an extremely effective way of terminating the Mini-Society unit. You will be amazed to see the prices received for goods and services when the students realize that their money is no longer "good" without Mini-Society. If some students had trouble understanding the concept of inflation during previous debriefings, we can almost guarantee they will understand the concept on the final day of Mini-Society when they observe in a most exaggerated form "more dollars chasing fewer goods."

G.   Consultants

You may wish to use older students, parents, experts in the community, and even yourself as business consultants. Often older children, as compared to adults, are better able to communicate business concepts and ideas to those within their general peer group. For example, allow the sixth graders from down the hall to consult with your fourth grade class. (Of course, the individuals using the services will pay for them in Mini-Society currency.) Or, if possible, neighboring junior or senior high students on tutoring release time may wish to be employed as consultants. They too would receive payment from buyers of their services. These older students have a certain advantage— the mystique of not quite being children and yet not adults. They have proved very effective in previous Mini-Societies and learn much from the experience themselves. In a thirty-minute meeting with the older students a teacher can brief them in terms of their roles and relate to them samples of businesses that have succeeded in Mini-Societies. (See Chapter 6 for a list of business ideas.) The teacher will find that children often are more in tune than adults with the types of goods and services Mini-Society students will demand.

You may be blessed with an abundance of parent aid. If so, take advantage of the opportunity to utilize parents' expertise. As with the others, parents should be instructed to charge for their advice. The major pitfall in the use of adult business consultants is that of ego problems. One rather famous professional economist's ego suffered greatly as a Mini-Society consultant because his advice was not as highly valued by students as that of a "lowly" teaching assistant who also had a consulting business. And parents have been known to become much more upset over the failure of their child's businesses than the children themselves—often because the business ideas in reality sprang from the parents rather than from the children. Sometimes a member of the community may have a special skill that a group of students, or even the entire class, may wish to secure. For example, one class hired an advertising executive to give them advice on signs and logos. They paid him fifty quets for his consulting and with this income he was able to buy four birthday cards, ten stickers, five book markers, a gymnastic lesson, and a dancing lesson—not a bad exchange for one hour of work. Other Mini-Societies have hired high-level bankers to explain how and why banks are profit-making institutions. Of course, the bankers were paid in Mini-Society currency. When using consultants, be sure to brief them on the general operation of Mini-Society, and remind them that they should charge for the services in accordance with market demand, etc.

You, the teacher, also may wish to open your own consulting business. Charge for your advice, but be careful not to push your ideas. Students may come to you for reinforcement of concepts from the learning centers, with general business questions, or to seek new business ideas. As soon as business is back on its feet, price yourself out of the market (let competing children take over) and out of a position that affords control over the shape of business in Mini-Society.

H.   Listing Ideas for Business Ventures

Each student can list one idea for a business venture in the interaction–discussion group, as homework, during penmanship, or in an art lesson (with an illustration to accompany the business idea). Provide "idea books" to help the students with this task. You may also wish to use copies of old Yellow Pages, department store catalogs, and magazines and newspapers containing ads. Remind the students that they are looking for business ideas that would be successful in the classroom; they are seeking goods and services that they can provide and that their classmates would be willing to buy. Reinforce the creators of good ideas; be especially positive in relating to children who have not previously been active participants in Mini-Society. Be sure they feel proud of their ideas. Often this idea-listing provides the necessary impetus to give business activity a substantial boost. Often, the students do not take the time to search for business ideas, do not know where to look, or simply need reinforcement of their ideas.

In this chapter you have been offered suggestions for facilitating business activity through the use of auctions, consultants, and having students list ideas for business ventures. We have found that in previous Mini-Societies these strategies have not only increased economic interaction but also resulted in positive side effects such as enhancing citizens' verbal skills, confidence, and self-esteem.

PART IV

DEBRIEFING MINI-SOCIETY EXPERIENCES: LESSONS BASED ON CASE STUDIES

CHAPTER 9

THE ROLE OF THE POST-EXPERIENCE DEBRIEFING SESSION

One of the most essential features of Mini-Society is the debriefing session. It is your job as debriefer to be aware of what transpires in the citizens' daily activities. Specifically, you will wait for an event to occur that has value in teaching about economics, consumer issues, careers, government, law, or values clarification. You will then review the event to obtain all the educational mileage that can be gleaned from it. Four steps are necessary in executing a successful debriefing. As the teacher you should:

Review   the details of the event. If a specific student is involved, she or he should verbally describe the occurrence from her or his vantage point.

Analyze   the economic and/or value aspects of the event. In this step you help the students identify the central issue or problem associated with the event.

Distill   the economic principles and/or value premises from the event. For example, if a student is attempting to decide whether to change his or her job, you would formally review the concept of opportunity cost in this step.

Integrate   the new information into the learning framework of the students. In this stage you will relate the new information to the students' current knowledge base.

Thus, during the operation of the Mini-Society, your role is that of observer, noting particular occurrences in the day's buying, selling, and other interactions that would be appropriate for debriefing. The students may also request to have a debriefing and may lead the session themselves. A debriefing session is not an open-ended discussion in which a bunch of unrelated questions are thrown at the students. A teacher skillful at debriefing can even go beyond what is achieved in successful inquiry-oriented discussions and can integrate new learning into the students' framework of analysis.

In the descriptions that follow, those events that have occurred frequently in over one thousand Mini-Societies have been synthesized into debriefings. These case studies are typical, and the suggested debriefing sessions should prove helpful in implementing them in Mini-Society.

At the beginning of a Mini-Society, when citizens select activities for which they will be paid, many believe that the more money they decide to have printed, the richer they will be. In the country of Starville, Tracy contended that citizens could solve *all*

Mini-Society economic problems at any time by allowing the teacher to print more money. She had many followers who thought this a unique and brilliant economic point of view. The teacher, envisioning her arm falling off at the ditto machine, became highly motivated to do a lesson on money and inflation to indicate that the wealth of an individual or country depends upon the amount of goods and services it can command. (See "We Thought We Could Get Rich Quick" in Chapter 10.)

Most teachers report that students become enraged as they see others opening businesses similar to their own. There are ardent cries such as "He stole my idea— you're the teacher, so do something!" Kelly, an aspiring entrepreneur, noticed almost as soon as money had been disseminated that the citizens had nowhere to put their money. She produced fifteen handmade wallets and sold them within the first ten minutes of Mini-Society. Because she had done so well the day before, she produced twenty wallets the next day and raised her price. However, Seth began to produce better-looking wallets, some of which contained a penny for good luck. Seth sold all his wallets and Kelly had to lower her price substantially in order to sell the wallets she had produced. She asked the teacher if it was all right to challenge Seth to a dual (since she was bigger than Seth). The teacher decided it was more expedient to do a debriefing lesson on competition versus monopoly—the effect of consumer prices–producer profits. (See "But It Was My Idea" in Chapter 10.) Even after the lesson, Kelly made a motion that only one of each type of business should be allowed to operate within the classroom. It was seconded by Terry, who had suffered competition in his snapshot business. The majority of the class, who were enjoying the effects of freedom of entry through paying lower prices, favored freedom of competition, and the resolution was defeated 23–4. This particular incident has occurred in one form or another in most Mini-Society classrooms.

Marlo and Luisa had been friends since kindergarten, and, three weeks into the operation of Starville, they decided to go into partnership and open up a beauty salon. They brought in supplies from home, school, and their neighborhoods, including combs and brushes, scissors, hair gloss, tongs, hair spray, clips, barrettes, bobby pins, ribbons, and various types of cosmetics samples. Before long they started arguing about business procedures. Marlo said Luisa was using dirty brushes and spending more time styling the boys' hair than the girls'. Marlo also said that Luisa was only doing three heads per Mini-Society session while she was doing six and that therefore she should get more of the money. Luisa maintained that she was providing "quality" hairstyling and was a better comber. Anyway, she stated emphatically, she brought in almost all the supplies, and it was only fair that Marlo work harder if they were to share the profits. Because they had not decided in advance how they would set up the partnership and what the responsibilities of each partner were to be, the bickering continued until the teacher conducted a debriefing. (See "I've Grown Allergic to My Partner" in Chapter 10.) They then decided on an informal contract, set up a corporation, and eventually brought in a third partner who owned a blow dryer. The problem of partners disagreeing is not unusual in most Mini-Societies. With a little teacher guidance through debriefing, most of the problems are resolved.

Phillip was a terrific piano teacher. He had his own very original method for teaching piano and charged twenty-five quets for a fifteen-minute lesson. Students were so anxious to learn piano that noisy lines were forming, and Phillip complained that he had no time to spend his money. "I have become a slave to my work," he moaned. Phillip, an acute observer of the economic process, had noticed that when the teacher was providing a fifteen-minute consulting service for five quets, she had resolved the problem of long lines by raising her price. But Phillip was already getting twenty-five quets for fifteen minutes of service. Was it fair to raise his price? Also, some of the students were complaining that Phillip had so many more people demanding piano lessons than could be handled that he was "cheating" and giving the lessons to his good friends. The teacher, realizing that this dilemma could face any of them (she had experienced it herself), debriefed the students on the rationing function of price. (See "Shortages, Shortages, Shortages; or Who Gets the Piano Lessons?" in Chapter 10.) During the lesson, in addition to describing the rationing function of price, she elicited suggestions on how to increase supply and reduce demand. Three days later Loren brought in a violin, Jerry rented a couple of harmonicas, and Linda started a jazz dancing class. Phillip raised his price to twenty-seven quets. There were no more lines, and Phillip even had some time left over to be a consumer. The students were later able to compare Phillip's situation with a major gas shortage and suggest some creative solutions that, perhaps, should be brought to the attention of Congress.

Norma faced a very different situation. She had started a stationery store and was charging ten saves for five pieces of stationery. On the first day of business she smiled warmly, and waited for customers. Only one customer bought her stationery. On the second day she continued to smile, and sold only two sets of stationery. On the third day the smile had turned to a semifrown, and she sold only one more set of stationery. Finally, she got an idea: she gave a free sample to Lucy, who absolutely raved about the stationery. Norma then hired Randy to make a sign that included all the nice things Lucy had said about her stationery. Other students saw the ad and ordered personalized stationery until Norma had as many orders as she could fill. The teacher used Norma's experience to show how advertising could increase demand and thereby increase profits. She also showed the students how to conduct a market survey to find out if a demand existed for their proposed good or service and at what price people were willing to buy the good or service. The class later converted their market surveys into demand curves and discussed why all their demand curves sloped downward to the right. They began to discuss the various ways to affect demand, emphasizing the effect of tastes, preferences, incomes, and substitutes. (See "How Do I Know Anybody Will Buy My Product?" in Chapter 10.) Students were having a little trouble understanding how changes in the price of a good affected the demand for complementary goods. Fortuitously, a situation presented itself in the case of Dan, who owned two tennis rackets and was selling tennis lessons on the condition the students provided their own tennis balls. When the price of tennis balls went up, the demand for Dan's tennis lessons decreased. Many disappointed business owners were encouraged when they learned to become entrepreneurs by converting into practice the principles of demand determinants.

Now we come to Roger and his rather painful experience. He had been making his own unique raisin-based health food mixture. After Halloween, when students brought in loads of candy, popcorn, and other delicacies, Roger declared bankruptcy. The class became horrified, because deep down they knew that the raisin mixture was better for them, and they really didn't want to see Roger's business disappear entirely. Simultaneously, Laura and Tracy shouted at the class meeting, "Let's give Roger more money. Right now he only gets six saves a package. Let's promise him fifteen saves a package and he can stay in business." The class thought this was a fair idea. The next day Roger came in with twice as many health food packages as he had supplied previously, but the class bought even less than usual at fifteen saves. Roger said that they had put him in a worse fix than before and said he would sell his surplus raisins. The students didn't like that idea, so they told Roger to lower his price; when the last Halloween candy had become stale two weeks later, Roger's business began to thrive again. The teacher used this opportunity to hold a debriefing session on price floors—differentiating between the effects of farm price supports and minimum wage laws. (See "The Case of the Unbought Raisins" in Chapter 10.) Over half of the students were able to relate Roger's experience to the real world.

Larry found out from his auditor that he had made more money than anyone in the class that month, but Larry was unimpressed. He was a jobber in the junk business, and his auditor told him he'd be crazy to change, because he was making so much money in the junk field. Larry, however, thought he could make even more money producing, selling, and racing cars. The teacher used this event to start a debriefing lesson on opportunity cost. (See "Should I Change My Job?" in Chapter 10.) He distinguished between accounting cost and profit, and economic cost and profit. The entire class soon saw that even if the difference between the total cost and total revenue were extraordinary, a business owner could still be experiencing an economic loss as long as he or she could be making even more money in some other business.

The question of whether to change jobs as well as the question of "to produce or not to produce" soon becomes a matter of considering one's opportunity cost. This debriefing should be repeated at least three times in a Mini-Society so that students can personalize cost-benefit analyses.

An inevitable error of judgment in any Mini-Society, and especially tragic in the country called Land of Intellectual Giants, is whether to hire a buddy. Emily, who made beautiful artificial flower arrangements, decided to hire Sandy, who rarely washed her hands, and worked excruciatingly slowly. Her redeeming qualities were her sweet temperament and the fact that she was in Emily's Brownie troop and her best friend. But it was costing Emily more to keep Sandy on than to do all the work herself. In addition, Sandy had an allergy and was constantly sneezing on the flower arrangements. The last straw came when Sandy demanded a raise. Denied, she complained to the teacher and gossiped about Emily. The teacher seized upon the opportunity to conduct a combination economics/values clarification debriefing session and to review the section of the circular flow diagram on making the decision of *how* to produce by figuring out the price/ productivity ratio. Later, he helped Sandy find her niche as a game center referee. The class used Emily's and Sandy's experience to discuss the idea of comparative advantage. Happily, Emily and Sandy revived their friendship and became good pals again. The real and often delicate question that plagues all aspiring Mini-Society entrepreneurs is thus not only what to produce but how to produce. (See "Should I Hire My Buddy?" in Chapter 10.)

Mr. Dash visited a Mini-Society class and became very interested in purchasing a student's original painting. He offered her two dollars for her artistic endeavor. She replied, "Your money is not accepted in our country, Frodoville; we can only accept hobbits." Mr. Dash went to one of the class banks to find out if there was an exchange rate. The student said, "We haven't gotten around to that yet." Mr. Dash asked if he could borrow some hobbits. The banker told him if she could get three felt-tip pens as collateral, she would loan him twenty hobbits at 10 percent interest. If Mr. Dash did not return the money within a week, the banker said she would sell the pens at the class auction. Similar situations arise in most Mini-Society classrooms. For example, in many schools, there are several Mini-Society countries, each of which uses a different currency. One class's currency may not be accepted in another class until an exchange rate is established between the two countries. When such situations arise, the teacher has a splendid opportunity to introduce a debriefing lesson on the role and functions of money in a society, including barter versus money. (See "We Only Accept Quibblings in Poohville" in Chapter 10.)

As students accumulate money for jobs and businesses, they soon find a box from home is not the ideal place to keep their money. This realization will often lead to the formation of a bank. Much later in most societies, bankers may realize that if they are allowed to keep the money for longer time periods, they can make money by investing it in classroom businesses. Thus, the savings function of a bank becomes a natural lesson. (See "Do We Want A Bank?" in Chapter 10.) The concept of central banking does not naturally evolve in Mini-Societies, although some teachers have embarked upon a discussion of the U.S. central banking system. Almost all of them have reported that students cannot understand more than the most skeletal concepts of central banking, and teachers have not repeated the lesson in their subsequent Mini-Societies.

In several Mini-Societies, students may prefer to keep their money in cigar boxes or small safes. It is not uncommon for a theft to occur. In fact, in one class, several students put mousetraps in their boxes to avoid stealing. One unfortunate boy became a victim of his own trap when he forgot to disarm it before excitedly removing his money for an impulse purchase. Most teachers have had measurable success in solving this problem through debriefing sessions, and stealing usually ceases in Mini-Society. (See "Is It Easier to Steal Than to Work?" in Chapter 12.)

Jerry, a Mini-Society citizen in the Valley of Friends and an established "A" student, tried to charge his teacher for correct answers to homework problems. The teacher responded by explaining to the class that there are certain acts one performs for nonmonetary remuneration. She initiated a values inquiry lesson on those actions people should do by virtue of their membership in the human race, a classroom society, or a family unit versus those actions one does for financial compensation. (See "Should We Charge For Everything?" in Chapter 12.)

In a few instances, a situation such as the following may occur. Some of the children in the UCF (United Class of Fonzies) were dissatisfied with the results of their business decisions. Sara, for example, decided to produce chocolate fudge. It sounded like a good idea, but it tasted sugary and she had a lot unsold. It grew increasingly granular and lumpy as the week progressed, and by Friday she was bankrupt.

Juan made science fiction drawings to stick on notebooks. He used all his spare time and produced over one hundred of the handmade stickers. Soon almost everyone had at least one, and Juan still had dozens left over. He complained that the teacher should have told him he had made too many stickers to sell.

Sara and Juan, along with some other children, made a proposal at the class meeting. They wanted the teacher or a class committee to decide what products should be made and how much of each should be produced. They argued that it would save time, prevent disappointments, and insure that everybody would sell all their products. Others in the class argued that they didn't want one person or one committee planning so much for them. They said they would rather make their own decisions and take the chance that they might be wrong or benefit from being right. The class defeated Sara and Juan's proposal. (One entrepreneur offered to give them business advice for a modest fee.) The teacher used their proposal to draw parallels between their society and the models of market and planned economics. (See "Why Are Some People Rich and Others Poor?" in Chapter 10.)

You will soon realize that most events that occur in Mini-Society provide opportunities for a variety of economic debriefings. For example, when Larry wanted to change from his junk business to a race-car business, the teacher chose to focus on the concept of opportunity cost, but just as easily he might have focused on accounting versus economic profit.

The following chapters are devoted to debriefing concepts derived from many events, some of which are not included in the foregoing description. Chapter 10 focuses on those studies most applicable to economic and consumer education, Chapter 11 emphasizes the debriefing of events relevant to government and law, and Chapter 12 concerns cases with implications for values clarification.

CHAPTER 10

CASE STUDIES/DEBRIEFINGS IN ECONOMICS AND CONSUMER EDUCATION

I. Should I Change My Job? (Opportunity Cost and Cost-Benefit Analysis)

A. Objectives

After studying concepts in this section, students will be able to:
1. Define opportunity cost as the alternative foregone.
2. Define accounting profit and accounting loss as the difference between total revenue and total cost.
3. Determine whether they have made a normal profit, an economic profit, or an economic loss, given a situation in which an individual's accounting profit is listed as well as the alternative foregone.

B. Economic Clarification of Ideas and Concepts

One of the most consistently encountered dilemmas in Mini-Society is that in which students have difficulty deciding whether to change employment or to change their business ventures. This is a problem particularly when students know they are making a profit and are fearful of making a decision that will leave them with less money. Concepts that figure in this decision include opportunity cost; economic profit and loss; and normal profit, accounting profit, and loss.

Each time any of us makes a decision there is a cost. The old expression, "there's no such thing as a free lunch," is often used but little understood. It deals with the cost involved in making any decision. If two students opt to play on the parallel bars during recess, the *cost* to them may be playing baseball during that same time. Because they cannot do both at the same time, if they opt for one they are giving up (it is costing them) the next best thing they could have done with their time. When you accept an invitation to a free lunch you are doing much the same thing. If your next best alternative use of that time is taking a nap, the lunch costs you the nap. This cost, referred to in economics as *opportunity cost* or *real cost*, applies to much more than decisions involving the use of time. When someone states, "This sweater cost me twenty-five dollars," what she or he is really saying is that the opportunity cost of the sweater was the next best alternative use of the twenty-five dollars. This person is giving up a lovely dinner that money might have bought. (When explaining opportunity cost to the students, it is important to note that the opportunity cost is *not* the sum of all other alternatives. If that were the case, most—if not all—decisions would be economically poor ones!)

In a Mini-Society, opportunity cost can be introduced when Bill decides to work as a teller in the bank for ten quets per week and puts his savings in the bank so that he earns an additional one quet per week. The opportunity cost to him may be going into business for himself using both the time and money he is now using to work in the bank and to keep in his savings account.

The concept of opportunity cost can be expanded into a method of analysis called *cost-benefit analysis*, through which students can explore economic profit, economic loss, and normal profit as opposed to the concepts of accounting profit and loss. Accounting profit or loss can be figured simply by subtracting total cost (all expenses incurred in the business operation) from total revenue (all money taken in). If revenue exceeds expenditures, an accounting profit has been made. If costs (expenditures) exceed revenue, there is an accounting loss. An example is Alice's Acting School.

Costs (expenditures) for the week

Employee salaries	25 elbers
Rent	10
Costume replacement	5
Props	5
Total cost	45 elbers

Revenue for the week:

Payments for lessons	40 elbers
Payment for entertainment at Parent's Night	20
Total revenue	60 elbers

Alice figures that she is making a *gross accounting profit* (profit before taxes) of fifteen elbers for the week ($60 - 45 = 15$). To figure her net accounting profit, Alice would subtract her tax payment from her gross profit:

Gross profit	15 elbers
Business tax	2
Net profit (for the week)	13 elbers

Alice is making the largest accounting profit in the class this week, but she is not content. When she realizes how good she is at figuring her own profit, she decides to change businesses. She will become an accountant and help others to figure out their books. How can Alice decide if she is making an economically wise decision? She can use the concepts of economic profit, economic loss, and normal profit in performing a cost-benefit analysis before making the move.

Alice now makes an accounting profit of thirteen elbers per week. She spends all her working time at the acting school. She has some savings deposited in the bank for which she earns an additional two elbers per week. If she goes into the accounting business, she estimates that she will earn a profit of eight elbers per week working part-time only. She can use some of her other time to work for the competing acting school run by Dennis to earn four elbers per week. Alice decides that she should leave her savings in the bank, but she also figures that she can earn an additional four elbers per week by renting to Dennis the costumes she has been using in her school.

Current earnings per week:

Profit from Alice's Acting School	13 elbers
Interest on savings	2
	15 elbers
	per week

Next best alternative earnings per week:

Profit from Alice's Accounting Service	8 elbers
Salary from Dennis for part-time work	4
Interest on savings	2
Rent from costumes	4
	18 elbers
	per week

Alice now earns fifteen elbers per week, but she could be earning eighteen per week in her next best alternative. Subtracting, we see that Alice (although currently earning an *accounting profit*) is earning an *economic loss* of three elbers per week (because she could do that much better in her next best alternative). If we change the figures so that Alice would only earn an accounting profit of four elbers per week from the accounting service, the situation is then reversed. In that case, she would be making an economic profit of one elber per week.

We can change the figures once more to have Alice earning five elbers per week in the accounting business. If so, she could make fifteen elbers in either case. When an individual is earning no more in his current business than he or she could in the next best alternative, we call this *normal profit*. When a normal profit is being made, the rational decision is *not* to make the change, assuming there is equal preference for either endeavor, because there is always a cost implicit in moving.

C. Activities

1. Ask a student who is considering changing employment to review the situation in front of the class. Have the student describe what she or he is getting out of her or his present employment versus what she or he expects to receive from her or his proposed employment.
2. Have the student calculate on the board her or his present income versus what she or he expects to earn from the change in employment.
3. Provide a hypothetical situation in which an individual is making (a) an accounting profit and a normal profit, (b) an accounting profit and economic profit, and (c) an accounting profit and economic loss.

    Example:

    To show an accounting profit and a normal profit, present the case of Virginia. She is currently a dressmaker and figures her yearly accounting profit as follows.

Total cost (thread, cloth, pins, needles, etc.)	$10,000
Total revenue (money paid her by customers)	$20,000

    Her *accounting profit* ($20,000-$10,000) is $10,000 per year.

    Virginia's next best alternative employment is as a flight attendant for an airline. She would earn $10,000 per year in that job too. Because she is doing as well in her current situation as she would do in her next best alternative, we say she is making a normal profit.

To show both an accounting and an economic profit, tell the story of Arlene. She is in business producing games for children, and this is her balance sheet for the year:

Total revenue (money paid for games) $50,000
Total cost (boxes, dice, markers, cardboard) $30,000
She is making an accounting profit of $20,000
                                                                                              per year

Arlene's next best alternative employment is teaching school, where she would make $12,000 per year. Because Arlene is making $8,000 *more* ($20,000-$12,000) in her current position than she could make in her next best alternative, we say she is making an economic profit of $8,000.

A person can simultaneously encounter an accounting profit and an economic loss. Consider the case of George, who is currently running George's Poodle Parlor.
George's Poodle Parlor Ledger:

Total revenue (for washing, clipping, and grooming dogs) $18,000
Total costs (for shampoo, scissors, and doggie nail polish) $10,000
Total parlor accounting profit . . . .$ 8,000

However, George could work at his next best alternative. He could change the Poodle Parlor to Hairdresser Heaven:

Total revenue (washing, cutting, and setting people's hair) $25,000
Total costs (shampoo, scissors, dryers, curlers, etc.) $10,000
Hairdresser Heaven accounting profit $15,000

George is earning $7,000 less accounting profit in his current business than he could be earning in his next best alternative ($15,000 − $8,000 = $7,000). We say he is earning a $7,000 economic loss.

II.   How Do I Know Anybody Will Buy My Product? (Market Survey, Demand, Risk Taking, and Entrepreneurship)

A. Objectives

After studying concepts in this section, students will be able to:
1. List and explain three determinants of demand: changes in taste, changes in income, and changes in the price of substitutes and complements.
2. Cite examples from their Mini-Society where changes in demand have occurred.

B. Economic Clarification of Ideas and Principles

The title of this section is a cry sometimes spoken but often hidden by young Mini-Society citizens. Many students would like to go into business or expand their current businesses but are reticent, because they fear failure. Determining whether the potential product will sell and whether a profit will be made is of great concern and can seem so overwhelming to students that it may prevent them from entering the ranks of entrepreneurs. These fears can be soothed in a debriefing on supply and demand, including determinants of demand and supply and the way in which these two interact.

The first step in determining the salability of a good or service is to determine the demand by using a demand schedule or market survey on the item. (See "Activities" portion for format.) Students also should be introduced at this time to the definition of demand and its characteristics.

Demand is a specific economic concept defined as "wants backed by the ability (willingness) to pay." Demand refers to the way consumers believe they will act in purchasing products at some specified time period; it is a *future* concept. Demand also refers to the range of alternative prices for an item. When taking a market survey or when determining a demand curve for a product, it is important to specify the time period being considered (tomorrow, for one hour, for the next week, for a year). It is also important to emphasize to students that they are being asked how many units they would purchase if the price for each were, for example, twenty quets and how many they would purchase if the price were fifteen quets (and so on for the range in which the entrepreneur is interested). They are *not* being asked how many units they would purchase at fifteen quets in addition to how many they would purchase at twenty quets per item.

In discussing why people demand differing quantities of goods at varying prices, emphasize that consumers tend to demand more of a product at lower prices and less of a product at higher prices. This is the "universal law of downward-sloping demand" and is true of the demand for *any* good or service.

Consumer demand for a good or service is determined by several factors. These are: consumers' personal tastes and preferences, their income level, the prices of complementary and substitute goods, and consumers' view of the future.

For example, Brian may demand more chocolate at all alternative prices than Jan demands because Brian likes it very much. He may demand less of the chocolate at all alternative prices than Alice because his income level is lower. He may demand less chocolate next week because the price of vanilla candy (a substitute) is low enough for him to switch to vanilla. Brian may demand more chocolate next week because he believes that chocolate prices will go up considerably next month.

When a demand schedule or market survey is taken, we refer to demand as the entire schedule (or resultant curve)—not to one isolated spot on the curve. As long as nothing happens to change tastes and preferences, income level, the prices of complements and substitutes, and/or the consumer's view of the future, the only movement of demand is somewhere along that curve. Such movement is determined by price changes alone.

When something does happen to change attitudes toward a product (in any of the four ways mentioned), we see a situation in which the entire schedule is changed; a new demand curve results. Perhaps Brian used to buy fewer chocolates than his friends because he thought they caused pimples. If he then reads a medical study convincing him that the chocolate doesn't cause pimples, he may be willing to buy more chocolates than before at all alternative prices. This is called an increase in demand. Demand can also decrease; that is, the entire curve can move on the graph to the left, indicating that Brian would be willing to buy fewer chocolates than before at all alternative prices. This was the change in demand anticipated by the U.S. government when it ruled that the surgeon general's warning be put on all cigarette packages. Thus far, however, this decrease in demand for cigarettes has not occurred in the aggregate, though it may have occurred for certain individuals.

Once potential Mini-Society entrepreneurs have determined the demand curves for their products among their classmates, they are ready to deal with the other side of the coin—supply. Supply refers to the willingness of suppliers at some future specified time period to sell differing quantities of their products at alternative prices. In a sense, supply is the opposite of demand. The universal characteristic of supply is that suppliers tend to be willing to supply more of a good or service at higher prices and less at lower prices. But how do suppliers decide how much of their products they are willing to produce at each alternative price? How do they decide whether to produce the product? They consider their costs.

In economic theory, the consideration of various types of costs can be quite complex. For Mini-Society purposes, however, the potential businessowners should consider all costs of production; that is, they should determine how much it would cost to hire labor, rent space, buy raw materials, rent or buy capital goods used in the production of their goods or services (e.g., a typewriter for a newspaper or a sewing machine for a purse company), and perhaps even how much interest they would have to pay on business loans. In addition, they should consider the cost to them personally (their opportunity costs) to determine if they would be better off in alternative businesses or employment. (For more on opportunity cost, see Section I, "Should I Change My Job?"). If the entrepreneurs can cover these costs (including opportunity cost to provide a profit as payment for the risk taken), they should produce.

C. Activities

1. Elicit responses from your class on different ways to determine in advance whether other students will be likely to buy your product.
2. Show the students how to conduct a market survey to ascertain potential demand. (You could take the example of Judy selling or planning to sell cookies in the Mini-Society. In her first survey, she could ascertain the class's two favorite cookies. In the second survey, she could find out how much they would be willing to pay for alternative amounts of cookies.)

    Example:

    At the following prices, how many chocolate-chip cookies would you be willing to buy on any one day?

Price per cookie	Quantity
$.20	_____
$.15	_____
$.10	_____
$.05	_____

    At the same prices, how many peanut butter cookies would you be willing to buy on any one day? (Do the same kind of chart.) After completing the survey, tabulate all the results and show the quantity demanded at alternative prices for both items. Use a demand schedule such as the one in the following example.

    ### Chocolate Chip Cookies

Price per cookie	Quantity demanded
$.20	_____
$.15	_____
$.10	_____
$.05	_____

In a lesson with the students, convert the demand schedule into a demand curve:

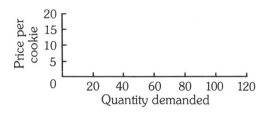

Next ask Judy to decide how many cookies she is willing to supply at the alternative prices. Have her compute all costs of producing cookies, including time, payment to workers, etc. Show the results of the cost analysis by drawing a supply schedule and supply curve (analogous to the previous demand schedule and demand curve). Determine the price and quantity on the basis of supply and demand. Figure out the anticipated profits.

3. Select a particular product in the classroom economy and ask the students to identify what factors would make them want more or less of the product (e.g., ice cream on a cold day and a warm day; after a pay raise or taxes; after the price of cones has gone down; before and after lunch).

4. Select any business that has experienced either dramatic increases or decreases in the demand for its product. Have the owner give a short report on what factors he or she thought caused the increase or decrease (e.g., advertising, tax decrease, or change in the price of a related product).

5. Explain the difference between a change in demand and a movement along the demand curve.[1]

6. Have the students construct a bar graph of the last two weeks of their sales records, showing quantity on the horizontal axis and time period on the vertical axis. Hypothesize the cause for any dramatic change in sales.

7. Ask the students to make up their own advertisements in the attempt to change taste in a variety of ways (e.g., posters, film strips, cartoons, newspaper ads, and radio spots).

III.   But It Was My Idea (Competition vs. Monopoly)

A.   Objectives

After studying concepts in this section, students will be able to:

1. Define competition and monopoly in terms of the effects on prices of goods and services within their Mini-Society.

2. List at least one example of competitive practice and one example of monopoly practice.

B.   Economic Clarification of Ideas and Principles

Getting a good idea for a business can be really exciting for a Mini-Society citizen, but seeing another producer of the same good enter the industry can be frustrating and disappointing, too. The concept of fairness enters heavily into any discussion of competition versus monopoly.

In our own society, we have laws against monopoly (when there is only one supplier of a particular good or service), but we also have laws protecting the original inventions and creations of individuals that allow them sole rights to the creation for a certain period of time (patents and copyrights). Are these contradictory? Some Mini-

[1]For further information, see Chapter 4 of *Understanding Economics: Overview for Teachers, Experiences for Students,* by Marilyn Kourilsky. Menlo Park, CA: Addison-Wesley, 1983.

Society citizens think they are contradictory, whereas others draw distinctions among the types of situations covered by these laws.

It is sometimes said that monopolists can charge any amount they want to charge and get away with it. This is not true. At some higher price, people will buy less of any good or service no matter how important it seems to them. At *some* high price people will stop buying altogether. However, monopolists do have a great deal of power over price within a certain range. If one is selling a desirable product, she or he needn't go out of her or his way to provide extra services or to treat the customers better than other sellers of the product: she or he does not have to lower the price to get business away from other sellers of the product, because she or he is the *only* one providing that good or service!

When one Mini-Society citizen starts selling a particular good or service and then another enters the industry (sells the same thing or a similar item), the situation changes. Suddenly, the monopolist has a competitor! Someone else is trying to get customers away. Perhaps several firms will enter the industry to sell similar products; they will all be competing for the same group of customers. They can do this in several ways.

Competitors can engage in *price competition*; that is, they can try to draw customers by charging lower prices for the product than others are charging. Most of us have experienced the effects of "price wars" at neighborhood gas stations, and many of us have sought out the lowest prices available in the area on a particular day of such a price war. Those stations were engaging in price competition, and Mini-Society entrepreneurs do the same thing. Not only is there a greater quantity of the product available to consumers (with several suppliers selling it and competing for patronage) but prices also are lower than they would be in a monopoly situation (because the businesses are competing for patronage by charging lower prices).

Other means of competition among businesses are referred to as *non-price competition* and include many of the "extra goodies" we have become accustomed to in our society. The major goal of non-price competition in drawing customers is to differentiate a product in the minds of the public. What matters here is not whether the product is "objectively" identical to other products (for example, whether it has the same chemical composition) but whether the customers think of the product as special or different from others. This can be accomplished through advertising and through special treatment of customers. The airline that advertises a "flub stub" for any customer who encounters a nonhelpful, nonsmiling employee is trying to convince people they will receive better treatment on their line than on others. Businesses that use recommendations of doctors or celebrities in their advertisements are trying to make the public believe that their product is better than that of the competition. Students in Mini-Society will do likewise, advertising a particularly friendly business, giving away balloons to customers, or using testimonials and statistics in an attempt to prove that they offer better service and/or a better product. The result of non-price competition to the consumer *can* be better treatment, although it can result in higher prices because of increased advertising budgets, and it may result in products of better quality.

Both price competition and non-price competition are in the realm of competitive practices. Monopoly practices also arise in Mini-Society, as they do in our world. These include collusion and price fixing. Sometimes one or more firms selling a particular product join together to limit entry into their industry by lobbying for specific laws or through practices considered "shady." Firms do this in an effort to keep prices up by keeping the sellers limited. Sometimes they will join hands to drive a particularly successful competitor out of business. They might even get together and agree among themselves to each charge the same price and not engage in competitive practices. This type of price fixing can result in higher prices and poorer quality of both product and consumer treatment.

Mini-Society citizens will want to consider the aspect of fairness in both competitive and monopoly practices. For example, they may decide to institute some copyright or patent laws requiring that a product must be changed in some way if it is to be produced or sold by an individual other than the originator. Or they may decide that the most creative work will be sought by consumers, and the problems will be resolved in the marketplace.

Students may wish to discuss fair versus unfair non-price competition. What kind of advertising is fair? Can producers advertise saying that their competitors' products are no good? Must they be truthful in the claims they make for their products? Students may also discuss collusion and price fixing. Are these fair practices? Some Mini-Societies have laws against such practices. However, Mini-Society citizens have been much more successful than we have been in controlling unfair monopoly *and* unfair competition practices through application of peer pressure, sometimes by boycotting products.

C. Activities

1. Review a specific problem within the classroom where, as a result of entry into the industry, a student received lower prices for his or her product or perhaps went out of business.
2. Give examples of ways of competing other than by lowering price (non-price competition). One suggested homework activity is as follows: All students have three T-shirts that they can sell for one dollar each. How are they going to make their T-shirts more desirable than those of their competitors? (Some will attempt to differentiate the T-shirts by tie-dying them, sewing on sequins, making see-through holes, or filling the pockets with artificial flowers made from plastic bags; some will do creative advertising; some will offer additional services or giveaways; and some will expect to sell on the basis of their own personalities.)
3. Ask students to illustrate examples of non-price competition from businesses in the outside community. For example, if your community is located near an airport, the ways in which rental car agencies lure customers can be compared and analyzed. Another example would be the way that savings and loan companies use "zero price" services to secure depositors (e.g., no service charge on checks written or a complimentary safe-deposit box).
4. Compare the ways in which hamburger businesses try to make their hamburgers appear better to children.
5. Ask students if they think it is fair to specifically name another product, and compare it negatively with one's own. (This discussion can help to clarify values.)
6. Role-play a situation in which there is only one manufacturer of a product and you are dissatisfied with it. Ask students what action(s) you should take. What would the manufacturer probably say to you? If there were other producers of the product (competitors), do students believe this producer would treat you any differently? Why? Be sure to emphasize the better quality you may receive when there is more than one alternative.
7. Now pretend that the foregoing situation is occurring within the classroom.

IV.   Shortages, Shortages, Shortages; or Who Gets the Piano Lessons? (The Rationing Function of Price and Economic Shortages)

A.   Objectives

After studying concepts in this section, students will be able to:

1.   Describe the rationing function of price.
2.   List three economic ways of eliminating shortage (raising price, decreasing demand, and increasing supply).

B.   Economic Clarification of Ideas and Principles

When the lines of patrons become unwieldy, who gets the piano lessons? Similarly, when the teacher is in business as a consultant and has more customers than she or he can accommodate, who gets the advice? Are we back to the beginnings of Mini-Society, again facing a scarcity situation? Obviously, the piano lessons are a scarce resource, as is the teacher's advice, but what we have also encountered is a *shortage.* In debriefing these situations, you must deal with several related concepts, including the for-whom-to-produce decision and the rationing function of price. Shortages result from legally imposed and self-imposed price ceilings.

The for-whom-to-produce decision is one of the three major decisions that must be made in the economy. All societies must decide in some way what to produce, how to produce, and for whom to produce. In a market economy, the for-whom-to-produce decision is made on the basis of price.

In a pure market economy (one in which no modifications are made by government), people get into the for-whom-to-produce group (they are able to purchase goods and services) by having sold their productive resources to firms previously; that is, those who have the money with which to buy are those who sold their labor, rented their lands, loaned their money (or other capital goods), or used their management skills as factors of production in the putting together of some good or service being produced by a firm. These people receive income for the use of their land, labor, capital, or management and so enter the marketplace with the money to purchase some combination of goods and services.

In a modified market system (most Mini-Societies are in this category), the government to some extent may change the composition of the for-whom-to-produce group. Tax money may be used to provide incomes for some who have not been able to sell their productive resources in a particular time period. Sometimes the government in a modified market will add to the incomes of people who have been able to sell their resources but are considered too poor to be able to live on their own incomes at an acceptable level. We see these types of changes in our own society in the form of unemployment insurance payments, social security payments, welfare, and food stamps.

People in the for-whom-to-produce group are then able to cast dollar votes in the marketplace (they can buy some of what they want). In a sense, price rations in two ways. Those who have price/productivity ratios most beneficial to firms are those whose productive resources are hired (see Section X, "Should I Hire My Buddy?"). Also, price rations the goods and services available for sale. Not everyone can buy all of everything he or she wants. People must decide what (and how much) they will buy on the basis of the prices being charged for the alternatives available in contrast to their own available resources—money.

Within the market, there is some demand (wants backed by the ability to pay) for the products being sold. The market price is the price at which the quantity of a good or service being sold is equal to the quantity people are willing to buy. When this market price is reached, those who are willing to buy at the price can do so, and those who are not willing to buy do not. A person may be willing to buy five hundred mink coats this winter (to carpet his or her floors) if they are sold at five dollars per coat; however, it is unlikely that he or she will be able to purchase these coats. The coats will be rationed by price (probably thousands of dollars per coat), and the person probably will not be willing or able to purchase the coats at this price.

Market price (equilibrium) has been reached when there are no unsatisfied buyers or sellers (everyone who is willing to purchase can purchase all he or she wants at that price, and sellers can sell all they are willing to supply at that price). In the case of people standing in line for Phillip's piano lessons or for the teacher's advice, we can guess that equilibrium has not been reached. Because the price of the services has been set below the market price, the quantity demanded at that price exceeds the quantity supplied at that price. This is the economic definition of shortage. Herein lies the difference between scarcity and shortage: scarcity is unlimited wants versus limited resources; shortage refers to a specific situation in which the price is not high enough to ration the goods and services successfully.

Shortages in Mini-Society can be caused by the suppliers limiting their own prices or by the imposition of a price ceiling (a legal maximum price for the good or service). Sometimes sellers are unaware of the demand for their products or sometimes they are purposely keeping their prices low to enable people to buy their services or goods. Occasionally, Mini-Society citizens pass price ceilings for certain goods and services in an attempt to insure that the "poor" can buy them.

When a shortage exists, the goods and services are rationed not only by price (for people still must pay) but also by another rationing mechanism. Most often, this is the first-come, first-served mechanism. People who got Phillip's piano lessons at first were those far enough ahead in the line to be served that day. We experienced a similar situation during a gas shortage crisis—those who got into line and were served before the station ran out of gas were able to buy gas. In some cases, people who were willing to pay a "time price" and wait in line for long periods got the gas instead of those who might have been willing to pay more money for the gas but couldn't spend the time in line. Additional rationing devices allow for discrimination on a basis other than income. For example, rent control is an attempt to insure that low income people can get living quarters at reasonable prices. This existed widely during World War II and still exists in some places today. But when a shortage of apartments exists (when the rent controls place the price ceiling below market price), landlords have many prospective tenants from whom to choose. This may indeed exclude many of the poor whom the controls were designed to help.

However, rationing on an additional basis other than price is one solution to the shortage problem. For example, in Phillip's case, some students suggested that he could get rid of the long lines at his piano studio by selling lessons only to his friends.

There are other resolutions to the problems caused by a shortage, designed to eliminate that shortage. (1) Demand can be decreased; that is, some method can be found to make people want less of the piano lessons at all prices, including the current price. For example, Phillip could have started to give "bad" piano lessons, making his product less desirable. He could have advertised that they were bad lessons. Also, Laura could have decreased Phillip's demand by offering a *substitute* service, e.g., violin lessons, flute lessons, etc. (2) The supply can be increased; that is, Phillip could provide more lessons at all prices, including the current one. For example, he could train more piano teachers to give lessons. (3) The government could step into the situation and subsidize the suppliers, making them willing to supply more of the product at the lower price. This is another means of increasing supply; however, it entails the spending of tax dollars for the subsidy. (4) The price of the product could be raised to the market price (equilibrium), where the quantity demanded is exactly equal to the quantity supplied. This is the solution used by both Phillip and the teacher who charged too little for her advice.

C. **Activities**

1. Ask the students to raise their hands to indicate how many piano lessons they would buy at twenty-five quets for a fifteen-minute lesson. Then sequentially raise the price by five-quet increments until no one is willing to pay the price. (Adapt this example to your own classroom.) In discussion, use this example to point out the universal law of demand—that as the price goes down, the quantity demanded goes up.

2. Graph a supply and demand curve and explain the concept of equilibrium price. Have the students discuss what will occur at a price below the equilibrium price (shortages and unsatisfied demanders).

3. Discuss with the students what might happen to the demand for piano lessons if they were able to take harmonica, guitar, drum, chime, song flute, or autoharp lessons. Illustrate graphically or numerically how this might decrease the demand for piano lessons.

4. Two of Phillip's star piano pupils decide to go into business. Show how this increases supply, and hypothesize what this will do to price.

5. Have the teacher make an analogy between the gasoline shortage and Phillip's problem. Emphasize that in economics a shortage indicates that at the price being charged, the quantity demanded is greater than the quantity supplied, and there are unsatisfied buyers.

6. Explain why Jerry, who was next in line for a piano lesson, was able to sell his place in line to Lindsey for forty quets.

V. The Case of the Unbought Raisins (The Rationing Function of Price and Economic Surplus)

A. **Objective**

After studying concepts in this section, students will be able to define a price floor as a legal price set above the market price, resulting in the quantity supplied being greater than the quantity demanded.

B. **Economic Clarification of Ideas and Principles**

What happens when the quantity supplied of a product at a particular price exceeds the quantity demanded at that price? What causes this problem, and what are the possible solutions? To analyze this situation we should concentrate on the two closely related concepts of insufficient demand and price floors.

In economics, a price floor refers to a legal minimum price for the good or service being offered for sale. Price floors can sometimes be self-imposed; that is, set in the minds of the suppliers. This price is somewhere *above* the market or equilibrium price (market or equilibrium price is the price at which the quantity demanded of the product is equal to the quantity supplied). The result of the price floor situation in which quantity supplied exceeds quantity demanded at a given price is a surplus—products are left over that suppliers cannot sell at the minimum price. For example, the price may have been set by the class in an attempt to guarantee a fair profit for the supplier of a certain product that the class believed to be socially desirable. The price also may have been set by the supplier to insure this same fair profit.

In setting a price floor, nothing is done to change the character of demand for a product. Consumers presumably demand the same quantities of a good or service at alternative prices that they would have demanded before the legal minimum price was put into effect. Disappointed entrepreneurs may approach the class with the complaint that the price floors did their business no good. They aren't making the kind of money they had hoped, because they have lots of their products left over. We can see an example of this same type of legal action in our own society with the minimum wage laws, which are an attempt to insure a fair wage for human labor. At the price set, demanders simply are willing to purchase less of the product than they would purchase at a lower price, and suppliers are willing to supply more at this new higher price.

In order to remedy the surplus situation created by a self-imposed price floor, students involved must reevaluate their situation and decide whether they are better off retaining the high price and being left with a surplus or whether they would be better off lowering their price to market price (the point at which the quantity they are willing to supply at the lower price is equal to the quantity demanders are willing to purchase at that lower price). They should also consider ways of changing demand so that the increase would result in a higher market price than before.

In the case of a legally imposed price floor, the situation is two-pronged. Presumably students thought carefully about the moral implications of their price floor. For example, they wanted to insure that a healthy food like raisins would continue to be sold in their country, and they felt that they must guarantee a certain price to the supplier to guarantee that he wouldn't go into the cookie business instead. Do they really want to repeal the law they so carefully considered? This may be the alternative selected. They may decide to let the supplier lower his price to the market price and hope that he continues to supply the desirable good at the new market price. They may advise him to advertise the benefits of raisins in an attempt to increase demand (change the entire demand curve so that people are willing to buy more raisins at all prices because they want them more). They might advise the entrepreneur to reduce supply to the point at which the quantity supplied at the minimum price is exactly equal to the quantity demanded at that price.

If the students decide that the law is one they wish to retain and wish to take action consistent with their judgment about a fair price, they must be willing to back this judgment with tax dollars. This can be done in several ways: (1) The government can pay for enough advertising and consumer education so that demand is indeed increased to the point where quantity demanded at the price-floor price is equal to quantity supplied at that price. (2) The government can subsidize the raisins supplier; that is, it can let him sell the quantity demanded of raisins at the new price and pay him not to supply more than that quantity. (3) The government can buy up the surplus raisins from the supplier and do one of three things with the raisins: (a) sell them to other classes in Mini-Society (dump them on the foreign market), possibly arousing the wrath of raisin sellers in those countries; (b) store the raisins for some future use, in which case consumers must not only pay for the raisins but for storage as well; and (c) give the government-purchased raisins to Mini-Society citizens who could not afford to buy them at the new higher price. (4) The government can subsidize the Mini-Society citizens who can't afford high-priced raisins by giving them the difference in price between what they can afford and what raisins currently cost, or by giving them coupons or vouchers with which to buy raisins (the seller collects on these from the government like markets do for food stamps).

In any of these cases, citizens must be willing to back their value judgments concerning raisins with tax dollars contributed by each working citizen. They also must decide if interfering with the rationing function of price is really worth the consequences.

C. Activities
1. Ask the student to whom the price floor situation occurred to report on his or her sales and how much surplus he or she has. Emphasize the differences between the times before and after the price floor was established.
2. Graph a price floor situation, and explain the reason for the surplus.
3. Have the students list the various ways to reduce the surplus (e.g., lower prices, the government will buy the surplus, decrease supply, increase demand).
4. Have the students give advice to another student whose parents have said that she or he cannot sell her or his pencils for less than twenty B.C.'s (which is far above the class equilibrium price).
5. For the more gifted students: Have the students do a homework assignment in which they compare the difference between a surplus caused by price support programs versus a surplus caused by minimum wage.

VI. Why Shouldn't I Cry Over Spilled Milk? (Supply and Sunk Cost)

A. Objective
After studying concepts in this section, students will be able to explain why a sunk cost is irrelevant to decision making.

B. Economic Clarification of Ideas and Principles

Students who have made "bad" decisions in their business or personal transactions may be quite upset. They may not be able to sell items produced for prices that will cover production costs (let alone result in a profit), or they may have purchased items they really don't want and can't sell for the prices they paid. These students are experiencing the dilemma of sunk cost. A debriefing on this topic should allow for analysis of how to deal with sunk cost. What should the next decision be?

The beginnings of a discussion may focus on what the students should or shouldn't have done. This is indeed crying over spilled milk. Once money is spent producing an item or buying one, the cost is said to be "sunk"; the decision has already been made and is irreversible. The same can be said of the action that doesn't involve an expenditure of money. The ideal situation, of course, is to recover that which is already spent, but what if that is not possible? Do we simply hang on to the item we have produced for sale or don't want for personal use and lament our fate? In nonpecuniary action (an act not involving money expenditure), do we simply shake our heads and give up? A rational approach may be to salvage what we can from the situation. In economics we refer to this as *minimizing our losses*.

To minimize one's loss in a nonpecuniary action may be difficult to explain. If one student fights with another and uses unkind names, the action has already been taken. Nothing can make the words go away, but often an apology of "I didn't mean it" can salvage the friendship. In a matter of sunk cost involving money, the situation may be more clear cut. Mike has produced Zingos for ten quets apiece, has sold most for twelve to fifteen quets apiece, and has two left over that he cannot sell for even two quets. He is facing a sunk cost dilemma. He may say, "But I spent ten quets apiece to make them. I *can't* sell them for less." Of course he can! But there are several considerations.
1. Mike may sell Zingos for as much as he can get for them, even if it is only one quet apiece or less. He may be losing money but he is not losing *as much* money as if he didn't sell them at all. He is minimizing his losses. In one instance, the student/businessowner is losing ten quets for each Zingo, or twenty quets in all. If the Zingos are sold for one quet each, the student is only losing nine quets on each Zingo or eighteen quets in all.

2. In some instances, students may feel they still should not sell their products at the present time. They may decide to wait until people are ready to buy more of the products (when the originals wear out), or they may decide to keep them for personal use.

    a. Using the previous example, we can see that if Mike holds the item for future sale, he *may* be making a wise decision. However, it is important to consider that he is still losing money, at least temporarily. If Mike can earn quets by selling the two Zingos now, the decision to hold them for future sale may mean that he is losing the use of the two quets at the present time. He might pay accumulating debts with the quets, but he may be losing in terms of what he could use the quets for in personal consumption (two quets worth of satisfaction), or he may be losing in terms of the interest he could earn on the two quets if they were put into a savings account or invested in another business. These alternatives should be discussed and considered.

    b. If Mike decides to retain the Zingos for personal use, he is also making a decision entailing opportunity cost. He should consider the worth of the Zingos to him personally in contrast to the use he might make of money he could recover with their sale. In making a rational decision about this, if he decides to retain them for personal use, then in effect he is saying that the personal use of the Zingos is worth foregoing the next best thing he could do with the two quets. (See Section I of this chapter for more on opportunity cost.)

C. Activities

1. Ask a student who has experienced a decision that involved sunk cost to describe his or her situation.
2. Give several examples of sunk-cost experiences in the society.
   a. Herman's father owns a Christmas tree lot. Each Christmas tree costs $.50 per foot. Herman's father is selling them for $2.50 per foot. On December 26, a man comes in and offers Herman's father $.05 per foot for firewood. Herman's father realizes that he is better off to take the offer than to refuse it. Ask the students why.
   b. People very often have garage sales. Even though they do not recover the original cost of the items, they believe they are better off than if they had not had the garage sale. Why?
3. Elicit from the students examples of sunk cost that apply to their own Mini-Society. Have them verbalize how they will use what they have learned about sunk cost in their future decision making.
4. Ask the students to explain that when their parents say, "Don't cry over spilled milk," they are introducing them to the concept of sunk cost.
5. Draw a cartoon of sunk cost.

VII. Do We Want A Bank? (Money and Banking)

A. Objectives

After studying concepts in this section, students will be able to:
1. Distinguish between the checking account function of a bank and the savings account function.
2. Describe how a bank is a profit-making institution.

B. Economic Clarification of Ideas and Principles

Of all the misconceptions about our economic system, those concerning the role and functions of a bank seem most prevalent among children. Many believe, for example, that banks are government owned and operated. They also believe that banks are in operation for the good of the community as altruistic ventures rather than as profit-making organizations. These misconceptions can seriously impede a child's understanding of banking services such as checking and savings accounts as well as loans. Understanding the reasons for banking services can aid in the understanding of how the services are performed.

Banks are private ventures owned by persons who provide useful community services that enable them to make a profit. Banks are not government owned but are connected to the government through regulations and procedures. They are controlled to some extent by the government organization called the Federal Reserve Board and deposit accounts up to a certain maximum are usually insured by a federal insurance agency. Special government agencies are concerned with the control and insurance of savings and loan companies.

It is in the interest of banks and savings and loan companies to provide certain services to community members (individual citizens as well as businesses). Providing services such as checking and savings accounts allows a bank to use part of the money on deposit for investment purposes; that is, the bank uses a portion of the money that customers have deposited in order to make loans and to invest in other ways. The bank earns a profit through the interest paid to it from these investments and loans. (Governmental control enters here in that the maximum percentage of deposits that can be loaned or invested is set for the banks by the Federal Reserve Board.) A credit-card charge actually involves borrowing money from the bank to be repaid at a later date. This is also true of the "ready reserve" service provided to customers, which enables them to write checks for more than they have on account at the bank.

Banks also provide other services such as selling travelers and certified checks, providing safe deposit boxes for the storage of valuables, aiding patrons in their collection of rental due on real estate, and sometimes providing help for depositors in preparing income taxes. Some banks give free gifts on the opening of new accounts. These are examples of non-price competition among banks. They are services provided to customers for free or for small service charges in order to draw customers to a bank. (For more on non-price competition, see Section III of this Chapter.) Although banks are permitted to engage in more price competition, they still find they can increase their profits by using the above techniques.

Two major services—savings and checking accounts—differ in several ways and are often confusing to children. They often see the savings function of a bank as commensurate with that of their own piggy banks. Initially, they see the "need" for a Mini-Society bank in the safety function it can provide. Discussion should center on two points concerning savings accounts. First, savings accounts are also called time deposits, because they are usually deposits made to the bank and left for a period of time. If necessary, U.S. banks can require a waiting period before withdrawal of the money is allowed. Banks do not usually do this, as it is not a wise competitive practice. However, we are seeing a rise in advertisements concerning certificate accounts (as opposed to passbook accounts) in which we are told that large interest penalties will be incurred in case of early withdrawal of funds from certificate accounts. This is because the bank depends on having the use of the money from a certificate account for a specified time period when it invests part of that money in loans and in other ways.

Why do banks pay interest to the depositors of these savings accounts? They pay interest because they are using the depositors' money to earn a profit for themselves.

They are paying the depositors for the interim use of that money. Some students will ask if this is a fair thing to do. Some feel that banks needn't pay for the use of the money, because the depositors weren't going to use it at the time anyway. The point to be made here again refers to opportunity cost. If the depositors didn't put the money into savings accounts, what else could they have done with it? They could have purchased goods and services with it, or they could have invested the money in some other way. For example, if Lynn deposits one thousand dollars in a savings account, the opportunity cost to her could have been loaning the money to her friend, Joe. Joe might have paid Lynn interest, but instead the bank is earning interest on her money while she does not use it. Or Lynn could have invested the money in a business directly or through the stock market, also perhaps earning interest. Instead the bank earns the interest that is potentially hers. Because she does not wish to take the risk of investing the money herself, she has put it in a savings account and allows the bank to use it. In exchange for this the bank pays *some* interest to Lynn for its use. She may be making less profit on her money than if she invested it herself, or she may be making more.

    Note: Some students will begin to panic when they are told that the bank uses part of their money while it is on deposit. They fear it will not be there when they want it. Explain the concept of insurance for banks if this panic occurs in your class.

    Checking accounts, also called demand deposits, differ from savings accounts in that the money may be withdrawn (a check may be written on the account) without a waiting period. While regulations have changed this somewhat, in general customers are not paid interest on the money in their checking accounts, because it is on deposit for short periods of time—the turnover in the money tends to be rapid. In fact, depositors in checking accounts are often required to pay a service charge (either blanket, revolving, or per check written) for the convenience provided them by this banking service. However, federal regulations do allow the banks to use a certain percentage of the demand deposit money for investment purposes, though this percentage is lower than that allowed for savings accounts. Checking accounts are useful because they allow individuals to carry with them their total deposit's worth of purchasing power without having to carry around all their cash. When someone with a checking account wishes to make a purchase, she or he can simply specify the amount she or he will spend on the check and indicate to whose order the check should be paid. Checks then represent the promise of the depositor that the debt will be paid through her or his bank on demand of the payee.

    In review, we see that banks provide community services in order to allow themselves the opportunity to make a profit. They do this by making loans and other investments they believe will result in interest paid to them. As an incentive to potential customers, they pay interest to those who deposit money in savings accounts and provide convenience to those who deposit in checking accounts, because the banks wish to use part of the depositors' money for their own profit-making ventures.

C. **Activities**
1. In a language lesson, have the students answer the question "What can a bank do for me?" You can then categorize their answers into the various functions of a bank—loans, savings, and checking—and discuss them with the class.
2. Ask the class to formulate a set of questions regarding banking functions and procedures (e.g., what might be the effects of regulations that would permit paying interest on checking accounts?).
3. Ask the students to write a letter to a banking executive requesting that he or she talk to the class primarily about these two questions: (1) How do banks make a profit? (2) How and why do banks use non-price competition to get more customers?

4. Create a learning center that includes the following: (a) How to write a check. (b) How to fill out a deposit slip. (c) How to fill out a loan application. (d) How to make a withdrawal. (e) How to compute simple interest.
5. Design an advertising campaign for a bank.
6. For gifted students: Have them research the difference between loans from a bank and loans from loan companies. Have them report their findings to the class.

VIII.   We Only Accept Quibblings in Poohville (Money)

A.   Objectives

After studying concepts in this section, students will be able to:
1. Explain that what gives money value is that it is accepted in exchange for goods and services.
2. Explain that in societies in which currency does not exist or is no longer accepted, trade (barter) is the method of exchange.

B.   Economic Clarification of Ideas and Principles

What happens when two Mini-Society classes with different currencies meet for international trade? What occurs when Elise tries to buy goods and services in Mini-Society with currency from her money game she has at home? What happens when parents or other visitors to Mini-Society try to purchase products with United States coins and currency? Students new to Mini-Society may say, ''We don't use that kind of money here.'' Second-term citizens may show their increased economic sophistication by indicating the exchange rate between the two currencies. We are dealing here with two basic economic concepts: the value of money, and barter as a substitute for currency.

Children have some common misconceptions about money, and we see some of these same misconceptions among the adult population. Many children believe that currency has some inherent value. To many, the value of a five-dollar bill is simply five dollars. In Mini-Society, students begin to understand that this is meaningless. The value of currency is seen in terms of the goods and services the currency will buy. This observation ties in with the concept of opportunity cost. When we say that a candy bar costs fifteen cents, we are indicating that we are giving up the next best alternative use of the fifteen cents when we buy the candy bar.

The misconception concerning the value of money is tied to another common set of misconceptions: that currency is accepted in exchange for goods and services because the government has proclaimed that it is money or because of the backing of currency in gold and silver. Discussion on this point should center on what really makes a money system work. Money is anything commonly accepted in a society in exchange for goods and services. It needn't have backing of a valuable scarce resource such as gold. Money is money and is accepted in a society because of the faith people have in it. If you accept currency in exchange for your teaching services, it is because you believe that you will be able to use the money to pay rent, buy food, put gas in your car, and go to the movies. In turn, the business people with whom you deal accept your money because they have faith that they can use it to pay for their factors of production, including their own profits. It is this faith that backs a money system in the true sense.

What happens when people lose faith in money or when no money system has been developed? People still exchange goods and services; however, instead of exchanging products for money (which they can then use to purchase other goods and services), they exchange them for other goods and services. This is called a barter system. Barter implies agreement between two parties that the things they are exchanging are of equal value. A barter system entails more time and effort than dealing with a money system, because parties often must search for an acceptable exchange or go through a long series of exchanges to get the items they wanted in the first place. However, there are certain advantages to a barter system, too. For example, when times are hard, citizens in a barter economy tend to produce more goods and services rather than fewer, as happens in a money economy.

Barter systems were prevalent among Americans during World War II. Citizens often bartered for scarce goods and services with their rationing coupons rather than money. In prisoner-of-war camps, the soldiers often used items such as cigarettes to barter for other things they wanted. In fact, cigarettes were so common as an exchange item in some camps that the cigarettes became money and were accepted in exchange for goods and services. We have seen throughout history that when currency is not available to or useful for people, they evolve barter systems to deal with their desire for exchange.

C. Activities
1. Using examples from your own Mini-Society, explain why you would not accept another class's currency in exchange for the goods you have produced. (Elicit from the class the idea that the other classes' currencies have no value in your class because other students will not accept them in exchange for goods and services.)
2. Have a representative from your class attempt to buy lunch with your class's currency. Tell the student to be adamant about the value of the class currency. Tell him or her to insist that the currency has value. (Meanwhile, apprise the cafeteria cashier of what you are doing so that she or he may explain to the student why the money is not acceptable.) Have the student report to the class about the entire incident.
3. A Goldville citizen had Xeroxed in black and white the class currency, which was on colored paper. The class refused to accept this counterfeit currency. Why?
4. Announce one day that no currency can be used, and instead have the students barter for the goods and services in their Mini-Society. Afterwards, discuss the way the barter system differed from their money exchange system. Were any students unable to negotiate a trade who would have been successful in a money economy? Why?
5. Role-play the following situation and resolve what effect it would have on the United States economy: By Golden Eagle Carrier Pigeon, news comes exclusively to your class that all the gold from Fort Knox has been stolen by Gold Thumb. Your class, in a conference, decides to tell nobody what has happened, not even their parents. Reenact the class conference, and then discuss why keeping the event secret would cause the situation to have no effect on the economy.
6. If the concept of money is still not clear within the context of your own Mini-Society, as an added reference you might show a film such as *Why We Use Money: The Fisherman Who Needed a Knife*. (Color; 10 minutes.) Learning Corporation of America, 1350 Avenue of the Americas, New York, NY 10019.

IX. We Thought We Could Get Rich Quick (Money and Inflation)

A. Objective
After studying concepts in this section, students will be able to explain why the real wealth of a country depends upon the goods and services it is able to produce as opposed to the amount of money it prints.

B. **Economic Clarification of Ideas and Principles**

Often in the course of a Mini-Society, the citizens decide that the way to have a wealthy society is for the government simply to print more and more money. It is this same more-is-better instinct that often leads the citizens to pay themselves large amounts of currency in the beginning stages of Mini-Society, when they decide on those few payments to first infuse money into the system. They have internalized the idea that more money (a greater amount of currency in hand) means greater wealth and purchasing power. Of course, if they decide to pay themselves in large amounts of currency in the initial phase of the system, price levels start out high. They have a relatively inflated money system, as demand is determined (at least in part) by the level of income of those doing the demanding. But what happens if the system is already in progress and the students suggest printing more money, perhaps as a way out of government debt? This situation most often occurs the first time students realize (or are told) that the treasury is depleted due to government expenditures and that, if they wish governmental services to continue, they must tax themselves to pay for them. Not enjoying the payment of taxes any more than the rest of us, the students look for a way out of the dilemma, and often the suggestion is to print more money. In debriefing this dilemma situation, we are dealing with the concept of inflation. The students will soon observe that inflation is caused by an increase in the money (multiplied by its velocity) while the quantity of goods and services available in their Mini-Society either remains constant or decreases—they see ''more money chasing fewer goods.'' The result of the citizens having more money to spend on the same amount of goods is that the price of the goods they want to buy goes up. They are now paying higher prices for the same package of goods and services because *production* of goods and services has not increased. Students will soon realize that their society is not richer, even though the government has printed more money. Like King Midas, they will ultimately learn the hard way that the *real wealth* of a Mini-Society depends on the amount of goods and services the society is able to produce and not on the government printing more money.

C. **Activities**
1. After the government prints a designated amount of money and the Mini-Society is initiated, record the average price level (i.e., during one week, record the prices of each item offered for sale and determine the average price of the item for that week). Then double the amount of currency in circulation and specifically show the phenomenon of inflation—a rise in average price level.
2. Take a survey among members of the class to determine four or five top-ranking wants of the students (goods or services they would like to have). Then divide the class into four groups, assigning each group a different income level: ten dollars, one hundred dollars, one thousand dollars, and ten thousand dollars (each individual in group A would have an income of ten dollars; each in group B one hundred dollars; etc.). Have each group indicate how much they would be willing to spend for each of the wants previously identified. How do the prices they are willing to pay differ in each group? Why?
3. Ask all the students to list what they would like to buy and what they would be willing to spend for those items. Give each student ten dollars more and see how many would be willing to spend more money for the same good, thus raising its price.
4. Have students draw inflation cartoons showing that one symptom of inflation is more money chasing fewer goods.
5. Auction off eight goods—two each of four different items. After the first four goods are sold, record the average price for each. Before selling the other four goods, double the money supply and then continue the auction for the remaining four

identical objects. (Do not tell the students in advance that a second group of identical objects is being offered.)

6. Choose one of the following products: mayonnaise, salad oil, peanut butter, bread, soap. Form committees and choose one of these products; have each committee trace the price of its product over the last few years. Students can do this by interviewing parents and storekeepers. For more gifted students, ask them to use the microfilm at the library.

7. Keep exact records of the culminating auction of Mini-Society, and (when Mini-Society comes to an end) conduct a discussion of the phenomenally high prices that were paid for the last few items. Emphasize that the reason students were willing to pay such high prices for these goods was that they knew the money would soon be worthless so they converted what money they had into goods or services.

X. Should I Hire My Buddy? (Price/Productivity and Comparative Advantage)

A. Objectives

After studying concepts in this section, students will be able to:

1. Explain that in hiring a resource, one must consider its cost to the producer, thereby including both price and productivity.

2. Explain why comparative advantage means people must specialize in activities in which they are relatively more efficient.

B. Economic Clarification of Ideas and Principles

With amazing regularity, students in Mini-Societies are faced with making friendship versus business judgments. An understanding of price versus productivity and comparative advantage can often help students involved in such a dilemma.

Price versus productivity is truly a ratio and can be understood through an explanation of the arithmetic processes involved. If one worker will work for ten dollars per hour and another will work for five dollars per hour, which should be hired? The answer is not clear, because there is not enough information. We do not as yet know how much we get for each dollar spent on the alternative workers (resources). If we are told that the five-dollars-per-hour workers can produce fifty cookies in an hour and the ten-dollars-per-hour worker can produce seventy-five cookies in an hour, the situation is more clear. Dividing price by productivity, we see that the five-dollars-per-hour worker can produce cookies at the cost (for labor) of ten cents per cookie, whereas it costs us thirteen cents per cookie for the labor if we have the ten-dollars-per-hour worker. But what if the five-dollars-per-hour worker can produce fifty cookies per hour, and the ten-dollars-per-hour worker can produce one hundred fifty? The situation is now reversed. (It will cost either ten cents per cookie or seven cents per cookie for labor, depending on which worker we hire.)

Comparative advantage can become a complex issue in economics and is most often spoken of in relation to international trade situations. But how does it apply to Mini-Society? First, in the least complicated way, the concept of "advantage" applies and is related to specialization. We all want to work at something that we can do well and that we enjoy. The issue of whether you should hire your buddy has two facets. Another question that should be asked is whether or not your buddy should work for you. Perhaps you run a bank and are thinking of hiring your buddy as an accountant. Your buddy is okay but not great in arithmetic, and, besides, he is a wonderful artist and would rather paint than add any day. In this case he would probably be better off (as would you) if he pursued his artistic talents through some other job or a business of his own. Not only would he probably be happier doing what he likes, but he would also probably be better at it and receive more recognition (pecuniary and nonpecuniary).

But what of the situation of the student who is "very good" at a number of things? How does comparative advantage apply here? Let us take the example of Shari and Jennifer. Both girls can produce picture books. Both also can produce paper dolls for sale. Shari is more productive than Jennifer at both of these. We say she has *absolute advantage*. But what about Jennifer? Should she look for still another alternative good to produce, because she can't compete with Shari (for efficiency) in either of these? Let's look at the balance sheet.

Shari takes ten minutes to make a paper doll, and Jennifer takes nineteen minutes to make a similar one. Shari takes fifteen minutes to put together the parts for a picture book, and Jennifer takes sixteen minutes to do the same.

Shari		Jennifer
15 minutes	picture book	16 minutes
10 minutes	paper doll	19 minutes
25 minutes		35 minutes

If both girls produce both picture books and paper dolls, Jennifer is spending thirty-five minutes to make one of each item, and Shari is spending twenty-five minutes to do the same. Is there any way in which the girls can be beneficial to each other (and to their Mini-Society) by becoming more productive?

Let's assume that they decide to specialize, with Shari making paper dolls and Jennifer making picture books. What will happen now?

Shari	*Jennifer*
20 minutes	32 minutes
(was 25) to make two	(was 35) to make two
paper dolls	picture books

Jennifer has what is called a *comparative advantage* in picture book production. Who knows? The girls may even join forces in a company selling paper products in their Mini-Society, because each saves time by specializing according to comparative advantage.

Thus, "Should I hire my buddy?" often becomes the question of whether, from a price/productivity point of view, it is wise to hire a friend, and from the friend's point of view, whether he or she is working at something in which he or she has a comparative advantage.

C. Activities

1. Ask a student to describe why another student, who is receiving a low wage, may still be reducing the profit (e.g., the student might not be too productive, might destroy the product, or might produce defective merchandise).

2. Have the students compute the following example: Dan can produce eighty pieces of thumb-print chicken stationery per week for a salary of twenty BC's per week. David can produce sixty pieces of thumb-print stationery for ten BC's per week. Carol can produce one hundred pieces of thumb-print chicken stationery at 30 BC's. Which worker should be hired and why? (Note: David should be hired at ten BC's for sixty pieces of stationery, because the employer will get more for her or his money.)

3. Have the students compute the following example: Terry owns a cleaning service, and business is expanding so rapidly that he puts an ad in the class newspaper to hire a helper. Two students apply for the job. Stephen will work for fifteen BC's per day and can clean fifteen desks during that time. Arnold will work for ten BC's per day

and can clean five desks during that time. Whom should Terry hire? (Note: Terry should hire Stephen, because it will cost him one BC per desk; if he hired Arnold, it would cost him two BC's per desk.)

4. Lulu and Stanley are in a contractual partnership making posters. Besides being the class's best speller, Lulu can form beautiful letters and fill them in perfectly. Stanley can outline the letters and fill in the colors adequately, atlhough he is not a very good speller. Explain why it might be wise to have Stanley fill in the colors while Lulu does the lettering, even though Lulu is better at both. (You might want to label this phenomenon as comparative advantage.)

5. Have the students role play Activities 2 and 3. In Activity 2, the employer's best buddy is Carol. In Activity 3, the employer's best buddy is Arnold. Carol is an excellent hair stylist and loves to comb hair. Arnold is a good carpenter and enjoys wood carving. Have each employer explain to his or her friend why both of them might be better off, both from a business and friendship point of view, if they did not work together.

XI.   Why Are Some People Rich and Others Poor? (Planned Economy vs. Market Economy)

A. Objectives

After studying concepts in this section, students will be able to:

1. Explain that in a market system, those who own resources most in demand will have greater income than those who hold resources less in demand.
2. Explain that the economic problems of what, how, and for whom to produce are solved in the market system by the interaction of demanders and suppliers.
3. Explain how the economic decisions of what, how, and for whom to produce in a planned economy are made by the planners.

B. Economic Clarification of Ideas and Principles

The question, "Why are some people rich and others poor?" plagues many Mini-Society citizens. Sometimes the students will equate wealth with being smart or good and poverty with being less intelligent or less deserving. Some will suggest that the resources of the country be divided equally among the citizens. Others will maintain that they want the right to make it on their own. In debriefing sessions concerning this question, the teacher and students should discuss comparative economic systems and the values underlying the different types of systems.

When discussing alternative types of economic systems, try to avoid value-laden terms such as capitalism and socialism. Many people, even young children, have emotional reactions to such words, often without even being able to identify the characteristics of such systems. Instead of capitalism, use the terms *nondirected economy, price system,* or *market system.* Instead of socialism, use the terms *directed economy, planned economy,* or *fiat system.*

The causes of individual wealth or poverty differ, depending on the type of economic system. Although we do not see pure examples of the model systems in the real world, let us consider the two types of economies at different ends of the spectrum: a pure price system and a pure planned economy. Economies in the real world tend more toward one or the other of these pure models.

If we assume that an economy begins with a group of people who value scarce resources held in common, we can logically assume that the resources will be used to produce what the group wants. In a small enough group, this might mean that every decision concerning the use of resources could be made by the group as a whole; that is, the value of common ownership of resources could be combined with a political system of pure democracy. This kind of decision making would be difficult in a large group. Imagine the entire population of a country assembling each morning to decide how each person's labor (a productive resource) would be used that day! Consequently, decisions would probably be made by a planner or group of planners. These planners might be elected (some form of a republic), or they might be self-decreed. The planner(s) would then direct the use of resources. In a planned economy, the planner(s) might attempt to direct these uses according to the wants of the population as a whole or might act in a more self-interested fashion. But even a planner with the common good at heart still faces the problem of scarcity. The planner must still select among alternative uses of productive resources in deciding what to produce and also in deciding the means of distribution of the output (for whom to produce). Hence we see that the phrase "from each according to his abilities; to each according to his needs" calls for value judgments about which needs are greater or more important than others. In fact, it calls for a judgment on what are "needs" and what are "luxuries." Such definitions may well differ quite widely from person to person. So in a planned economy, an individual wanting clothing, another wanting entertainment, a child wanting toys, and even a diabetic wanting insulin are each dependent on the judgments of the planner to have their wants satisfied and to be identified as needing the resource.

In real-world economies tending toward this model, planners decide what to produce, and there is a differential in the incomes of those whose labor is hired to do this production. This group of people can then purchase items that are available to them in stores. They have consumer freedom (they can choose among alternatives to purchase) but do not have consumer sovereignty (they cannot, by their purchasing, determine what will be produced in the next production cycle). Their levels of income are determined by a planning process, and hence their comparative wealth or poverty, in the long run, is determined by the planners. Ownership of personal property is allowed but ownership of productive means is not; that is, individuals are not allowed to go into business for themselves, hiring labor and other productive resources. A drawback of such a system is that individuals are not at liberty to take the risk of entrepreneurship and realize profits from this risk. A benefit of such a system is that individuals are more likely to be provided with jobs through which to earn income and purchase some of their wants; that is, they will be more assured of some form of security.

If we assume that an economy begins with a group of people who value scarce resources owned privately by individuals, we can logically assume that individuals will use these private resources to produce what they want. Individuals will eventually realize that specialization is advantageous in that people can produce what they are best at producing (which others want and will pay for) and trade these items with other specialists to satisfy their own wants. Specialists providing what others want and are willing to pay (or trade) for would become the successful ones. What of specialists whose products weren't highly desired by others? They would not be as successful and eventually might have to change their products or hire their productive resources out to other producers. A price system would develop, with the prices of products directing them into and out of higher-valued uses. For example, we already know that at lower prices, people would tend to shoe their horses more often (buy more blacksmith services). But in addition to this, at very high prices, blacksmith services might be used only for shoeing horses, whereas at lower prices, people might hire the blacksmith to make "less important" items such as children's toys.

In a system where the use of money as a medium of exchange had developed, those who are comparatively wealthy would be those whose factors of production were more in demand (labor, land, capital, and entrepreneurial abilities). This is determined in a price system by the demands of the consumers (what to produce) interacting with the decisions of producers on how to produce. Those whose resources were in demand according to this combination would earn money with which to satisfy their wants.

In real-world economies tending toward this type of price system model, in the long run consumers determine what is produced by their purchasing of goods and services. In other words, if consumers won't buy a product at a price that allows the producer to cover costs, the producer will eventually go out of business or change her or his product to meet consumer demands. Because producers decide what to produce in this manner and then decide how to produce based on price versus productivity of available resources, those whose resources are appropriate to the particular industry and are cost-effective will be hired. The success or failure of individual entrepreneurs is then dependent on the judgments of consumers as to what they want and are willing to pay for. The success or failure of those in the factor market (selling their land, labor, etc.) is also in part determined by the consumers and in part by the producers' judgment of their cost-effectiveness. In the real-world economies tending toward this type of model, the what-to-produce and for-whom-to-produce decisions sometimes are modified by government. For example, if citizens in a representative system feel a particular industry produces an undesirable good or service, they can appeal to their representatives to tax the industry highly or take other measures to discourage participation. This may be initiated by the legislators themselves or by special-interest groups. In a pure democracy, presumably such modification of the for-whom-to-produce decision is achieved through such means as subsidies to those who were unable to sell their factors of production (or who were unable to sell enough for a particular standard of living). Many other measures are also used to modify the what-to-produce and for-whom-to-produce decisions, but in a price system, the consumer basically determines the long-run wealth or poverty of individuals by their buying behavior. A drawback of this type of system is that some very desirable products may not be produced, because consumers will not buy enough of them at a high enough price to make production worthwhile. Also, some very talented or skilled people may not be able to find work in their specialties, because they are not in demand in the factor market. However, an advantage of such a system is that each individual can make an attempt to sell his or her resources as he or she sees fit, allowing him or her to take a risk and possibly make a large profit.

In discussing comparative economic systems with intermediate-level students, it is important to emphasize that an opportunity cost (tradeoff) exists between the two types of systems. One's personal values enter highly into which type of system is preferred. Basically, these values are those of security versus individual freedom.

C. **Activities**
1. Present the circular flow diagram to the students, and explain how the decisions of what, how, and for whom to produce are made in a market system. (Note: Description of this diagram is in many social studies texts, including *Understanding Economics: Overview for Teachers, Experiences for Students,* by M. Kourilsky. Addison-Wesley, 1983.)
2. Emphasize the relationship of the circular flow diagram and the concept of private property.
3. Describe the main features of the market system model, and have the students identify to what degree the essential features of a competitive market are prevalent within their own Mini-Society (e.g., freedom of entry and exit, perfect knowledge of market conditions, homogeneity of product, consumer sovereignty, etc.).
4. Explain the main features of a planned economy, and explain how the decisions of what, how, and for whom to produce are made within the system.

5.   Distribute the following problems to the class:
        a. You own one-thirtieth of the tissue paper in the art cupboard. Each member of the class also owns one-thirtieth of this tissue paper. You think it should be used for laminating bottles. Whom must you convince? How will you do it? How will you all decide who gets the finished products? What kind of economy is this most like?
        b.   You own four sheets of tissue paper. You want to use it for laminating bottles. Whom must you convince? How will you decide who gets the finished products? What kind of economy is this most like?
        Choose two students who have correctly identified the economies to role play their solutions.

CHAPTER 11
CASE STUDIES/DEBRIEFINGS IN GOVERNMENT AND LAW

I. Introduction

In the following five debriefings, students will evaluate different forms of government, in addition to judicial and legal alternatives in order to discover the options that exist for them within their society.[1]

As an introduction to these debriefings, you may wish to remind your students that in Mini-Society they have come to a point where they may want some rules for all citizens to follow. They will probably need to discuss:

1. Who will have power?
2. Who will make the rules and decisions?
3. How might their society be arranged or organized?

Students can get some ideas for their society by looking at different kinds of governments that exist in the world. Remind the citizens, though, that they can create any type of Mini-Society they want, and that includes the form of government they choose to have, if any. Also, be sure not to introduce these debriefings until incidents have occurred that necessitate a decision of alternative types and forms of government.

Sample chart or bulletin board. (Drawings are from Figures 11–2 and 11–3.)

Figure 11–1

[1](See Figure 11–1 for a sample chart or bulletin board to use in conjunction with these debriefings.)

II. Who Will Have a Say? (Democracy vs. Dictatorship)

A. Objective

After studying concepts in this section, students will be able to differentiate between a democracy and a dictatorship, citing examples of each.

B. Activities

1. Initiate class discussion by asking, "If we decide to make rules, what are the different ways we can make them?" (Try to elicit the following answers.)
   a. All people make (suggest) rules and vote.
   b. People vote for others to make rules for them.
   c. A small group (not selected through voting) makes the rules for everyone.
   d. One person makes the rules for everyone.

   Continue by asking, "Does anyone know what we call the 'a' and 'b' forms of making rules?" (Answer: democracy or republic). "Does anyone know what we call the 'c' and 'd' forms of making rules?" Answer: dictatorship).

   Further clarify these terms for students:

   Democracy is a government by the people. *Dictatorship* is a government in which the power is held by one person or a small group of people.

2. Pose the question "What are some good and bad points of each system?" Possible responses might include:
   a. In a democracy, everyone gets an opportunity to voice an opinion, so a broader range of input is possible. Everyone gets an equal say or voice in the rules. (Pros)

   In a democracy, it is often necessary to compromise in order to reach a decision. It might take longer to decide on important issues or make rules, because everyone can add input before voting. (Cons)
   b. In a dictatorship, it might take less time to make the rules or decisions, because a few people decide. (Pros)

   In a dictatorship, all of the people may not be represented, or all may not get an opportunity to suggest ideas. Dictatorships do not give everyone an equal say in making rules. (Cons)

3. Ask the class, "Is a dictatorship always bad?" No. The difference between the two is not really a moral issue. A dictator may have the best interests of the people in his or her plans and thus be a "benevolent dictator." Also, the dictator might just be the brightest and the smartest in the society and truly know what is best for everyone. Remember that there are good and bad points to both systems.

4. Using Figures 11–2 and 11–3 as ideas for a bulletin board display, discuss, and have students identify each form of rule making.

5. If you have emphasized current events in the classroom, suggest the following options for fifth- and sixth-graders:
   a. Discuss current examples of dictatorship and democracy.
   b. Discuss how dictatorships come to power. You may want to introduce the concepts of force, military coups, and the exercise of propaganda.

6. Read and discuss "KneeHi and the Weefolk," found in this chapter.

Figure 11–2

Figure 11–3

KneeHi and the Weefolk

There once was a society of weefolk—not one was over twenty inches tall. They were all very friendly, and each weeperson ran a business in town.

Occasionally, weefolk would have disagreements. Once in a while the group would have to make a decision or make some rules in order to have things run smoothly. You know, weefolk were a temperamental bunch, and they liked having certain rules for everyone to follow.

When it came to making rules for the society, all of the weefolk had their own ideas, but they would let KneeHi, the smartest weeperson of all, make the final decisions. Usually they would all come together in

a weeperson

a meeting, and each weeperson in turn would speak her or his piece. Then KneeHi would clasp his hair, grasp his head,

KneeHi clasping his hair

and exclaim, "Well, in the interest of the group, I have decided . . .!" And that is how all decisions were made in the land of the weefolk.

Do you think the weefolks had a good way of making decisions? Would you call this a democracy or dictatorship? Why?

Discussion: Because KneeHi made all the decisions, the weefolk's society was a dictatorship—a benevolent dictatorship, because it was assumed that KneeHi listened to all the ideas and then decided in the best interest of the group.

But it might be argued that the weefolks had a type of democracy, because each weeperson had his or her turn to voice an opinion. KneeHi probably took a concensus of the group and decided what the majority wanted.

This story is a good lead-in to the next debriefing on pure democracy versus republic.

III.   Do I Get To Raise My Hand This Time? (Pure Democracy vs. Republic)

A.   Objective

After studying concepts in this section, students will be able to differentiate between a pure democracy and a republic, citing characteristics of each form of government.

B.   Activities

You may want to begin by defining the two forms of democracy as follows.

Pure democracy   is a government whose motto is "one person, one vote"—the majority wins decisions.

Republic   is a government in which representatives selected by the larger group vote for their constituents. (Representatives usually are elected by the group but may be appointed or selected at random.)

1. Discuss the question "What do you think might be some strengths or weaknesses of each system?" Possible responses might include:
    a. A strength of a republic is that it may be more efficient; that is, it may take less time to reach a decision. A large voting group is very cumbersome. Democracy in its pure form works best with a smaller group.
    b. Another strength of a republic is the belief that sometimes the speed at which a decision is made is crucial to the success of that decision.
    c. A weakness of a republic is that the representatives may not vote in the interest of the majority of the people they represent. They may vote according to their personal self-interests.
    d. Another weakness of a republic is that, in reality, people have no assurance that the representatives will vote as they say they will.
    e. Another possible weakness of a republic is that not all of the opinions may be proposed to the group at large, because people usually voice their opinions to the representatives only.
2. As an exercise, have the group make the same decision twice, and compare the systems and the results.
        Example: Have the class decide what sport to play during physical education period.
    a. (Republic) Select representatives for small sections of the class (randomly out of a hat or through an election, if there is time). Give the sections (constituents) several minutes to make their wishes known to the representatives. Then have the representatives vote aloud.
    b. (Pure Democracy) Have the class nominate or suggest several choices, and then take a vote at large. Majority wins. (Note: This will work best if the class has many differences of opinion.)
    When the decisions have been made, ask the students what the differences were. Which form did they like best? Why? Did they feel well represented the first time? What were some advantages and disadvantages of each procedure?
3. If you have access to other classes in the school, you might wish to use the following example, which is designed to highlight the practical advantages of a republic.
    a. Ask the students in each of the classes to decide what would be the best way to choose a school mascot or school color. They may decide to let each student in the school vote or choose to have each classroom elect a representative to vote for their class.
    b. Discuss the differences in the selection procedure and the advantages and disadvantages of each.

IV.   Can the President Do That? (Presidential vs. Parliamentary Executive Branches)

A. Objective
After studying concepts in this section, students will be able to explain in their own words the differences between a presidential and a parliamentary system.

B. Clarification of Ideas
(To achieve maximum clarity, a brief discussion of the branches of government should precede this debriefing.)
        In world government, there are usually three groups of power or three different branches of concern.
1. Lawmakers (legislative branch).

2.   Law executers (executive branch)—put laws into effect.
3.   Law judgers and enforcers (judicial branch)—interpret the law.
Ask students, "What are the three groups called in the United States?"
1.   Legislative branch: Congress (House of Representatives and Senate).
2.   Executive branch: president and advisers.
3.   Judicial branch: Supreme Court and all lower courts.

In Mini-Society, students may not want to have a leader or this much
organization. But it is interesting to see how these groups work in the world. Students can
get some ideas for their society if they decide to operate their society in a similar way.
Remember, this is how other societies work. Students can make their society work in any
way they want.

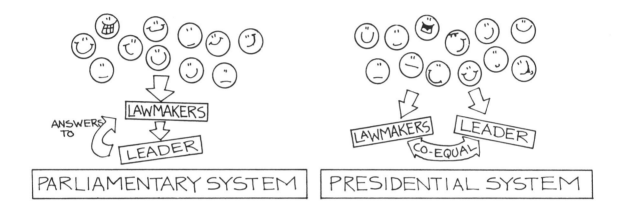

Figure 11–4

(You may wish to draw a diagram similar to Figure 11–4 on the chalkboard or a chart.)

If the executive leader is chosen by the lawmakers (who are elected by the
people), we call the system parliamentary. If the leader of the executive branch is chosen
directly by the people and is responsible to the people, we call the system presidential.

In a parliamentary system, the leader is responsible to the lawmakers to whom
he or she answers. Although the executive leader is chosen by the lawmakers, he or she is
chosen from a group of lawmakers who are elected by the people. Thus, the people
know that when they elect the lawmakers, one of them will become the leader of the
group.

In a presidential system, the lawmakers and the leader answer to the people who
elected them to office. In a sense, they are co-equal. One does not have more power than
the other; they can check up on each other.

The chief executive of a parliamentary system is responsible to the group that
selected her or him; that is, the lawmakers. On important issues, the executive will
probably agree with a majority of the parliament. If the chief executive does not agree
with the majority, that person may be terminated (fired, recalled). After all, the executive
was selected by a majority of the lawmakers. In a parliamentary system, a group of
people (lawmakers) watching over the decisions of the executive leader is a check on the
power of the executive leader.

In a presidential system, the president and the lawmakers are equally responsible
to the people. Because they were both chosen freely by the people, the two branches do

not always have to agree on important issues. This provides a "check and balance" system of power. This system sometimes makes the decision-making process a long affair, especially if the two groups are always in disagreement.

C. Activities
1. Lead a discussion using the following questions to amplify the students' understanding of the two systems.
   a. If the lawmakers choose a leader, do you think the leader will be as free to make decisions as if the people chose the leader directly?
   b. Will the leader in a parliamentary system want to please the lawmakers? How will this affect his or her decisions?
   c. Can the leader in a parliamentary system criticize the lawmakers? If so, do you think such criticism might be risky?
   d. If a leader is chosen by the people, is it risky for the leader to criticize the lawmakers?
   e. If the leader is chosen by the people, how can the leader check up on the lawmakers?
2. Have the students draw a cartoon that depicts the two systems—parliamentary and presidential. In their cartoons, they should try to show which of the two they believe is more desirable for their Mini-Society.

V.   But I Didn't Do It, Just Ask My Friends! (Trial by Judge vs. Trial by Jury)

A. Objective
After studying the concepts in this section, students will be able to explain the difference between a trial by judge and a trial by jury.

B. Clarification of Ideas
An old saying goes, "Rules are made to be broken." If a society has lawmakers and law executers (people to carry out the laws), is everything going to run smoothly? Aren't laws or rules sometimes broken? Don't things sometimes happen that require a third party to suggest a fair remedy or solution to the problem?

Laws and rules are sometimes broken, not always intentionally. Sometimes things happen in the normal course of running Mini-Society that cause disagreements between people. Other times things happen quite by accident. Many times a society will need someone to interpret the law or the situation.

C. Activities
1. Lead a discussion using the following questions to increase the students' understanding of the judicial system.
   a. Have you ever been accused of doing something that you didn't do or didn't

mean to do? How did you feel? What did you do about it?

b.   What do the terms *guilty* and *innocent* mean?

c.   If someone is accused, is that person always guilty?

d.   In a society, when someone is accused of breaking a rule or there is a situation to be remedied between several parties, two basic decisions must be made. What are these?

    (1)   Establish whether the rule was broken or to what extent the person accused was responsible. Guilty or innocent?

    (2)   If the person is responsible, how can the situation be remedied?

e.   When someone is accused of breaking a law or of doing something wrong, what might Mini-Society citizens do?

    (1)   They might have a trial or a discussion to determine if the person is responsible.

    (2)   Discuss the concept of a trial. Decide with the group what will go on at a trial. You may want to discuss the concepts of proof and evidence.

f.   At the trial, who will finally decide if the person is responsible for breaking the law?

    (1)   A group of citizens (peers) could listen to the trial and vote. These people could be selected at random or could be appointed. This is called a jury.

    (2)   One "expert" or a panel of experts could listen to the trial and decide. These people are called judges.

    (Note: The students will probably view an "expert" as a very fair person. You will probably want to discuss the qualifications of the judges and how they could be selected. Discuss also how the jury could be selected.)

g.   Do you think an accused person should be able to choose whether he or she wants a jury or a judge to decide?

h.   If the person is found responsible (guilty), the next decision is, "How might the situation be remedied?" Should the judge or the jury decide?

2.   Have the students list the good and bad points of each of the judicial methods. Compare answers. Their responses might include the following:

    A judge is only one person. She or he may have unconscious biases; however, this person should be an expert in interpreting the laws. This person is usually more fair than citizens in certain instances, because she or he has had more experience in interpreting the law and can remain more objective.

    A jury gives a wider representation of feelings and thoughts, because it is composed of several people. Because it is a peer group, a jury may be more understanding, but the people may also get caught up in the emotion of the situation. They are not experts like the judge.

3.   Create a bulletin board or display of how the judicial branch functions, and discuss it with the class. (See Figure 11–5 for a sample display.)

4.   Read the story in this chapter called "All Eyes Turned to Grant," and discuss the decision.

Sample of an optional chart for bulletin board and or discussion.

Figure 11–5

All Eyes Turned to Grant

One Wednesday in Mini-Society, while moving some boxes of supplies to his art store, Grant accidentally knocked down Susan's sign to her Boogie Dance Parlor. Grant was not extraordinarily clumsy, but he was carrying a lot of boxes and didn't see the sign.

When Grant realized what he had done, he quickly picked up the sign and put it back in place. Because he was in a hurry to get started before Mini-Society period ended, he really didn't examine the sign to see if it had been damaged. He assumed that it was okay. Three people witnessed the incident, but because nothing seemed unusual, they continued on their way and about their business without saying anything.

During the group meeting at the end of Mini-Society period, Susan announced, "Someone has damaged my Boogie Dance Parlor sign. The corner is broken off!"

"Hey, I saw Grant breaking her sign," said John from the corner.

"No, you saw me just picking it up off the floor," explained Grant quickly.

"I think Grant should buy me a new sign or make a new sign for me," complained Susan.

All citizens' eyes turned to Grant. There was silence in the room. What would *your* society do?

Epilogue: Grant immediately demanded to have a trial, and the class agreed. A group of jurors was selected after Grant decided to have a trial by jury.

After all the evidence was presented at the trial, the jury decided that in accidentally knocking over Susan's sign, Grant probably had broken off the corner. But because neither Grant nor the three witnesses had actually seen if the corner was broken, the jury decided to have Grant pay only for one-third of Susan's new sign.

VI. I've Grown Allergic to My Partner! (Specialization, Gentlemen's Agreements, and Legal Contracts)

A. Objectives

After studying concepts in this section, students will:
1. Negotiate a contract or gentlemen's agreement.
2. Agree, as partners, on their area of specialization before entering a contract.

B. Clarification of Ideas and Principles

In the dilemma of students growing "allergic" to partners, they may tentatively conclude that, because it has been a problem for them to work with other students, they should simply work alone. They may ask, "Why work with anyone else to begin with? It only causes problems." In debriefing this dilemma, you are dealing with the economic concept of specialization as well as with the concept of a legal contract versus a gentlemen's agreement. (For specialization, see also "Should I Hire My Buddy?" in Chapter 10, which is a discussion of comparative advantage.)

The concept of specialization is also one of efficiency. People work with others (specialize in a particular business or task within a business) based partly on what they are good at and also on what they like to do, but are there other reasons? What would happen if each person in a society produced (or tried to produce) all the goods and services she or he personally wanted? It is difficult if not impossible to imagine people in our own society providing their own steel, food, medical services, and educational services. Even in a Mini-Society, with each citizen attempting to provide his or her own chocolate-chip cookies, perhaps, as well as paper-bag puppets and knitting lessons, we can see difficulties arising. Some goods and services might be available only to those with the expertise to produce them. Some might not be available at all. In any case, production would take up all the citizens' time, eliminating leisure for playing games and so forth. Specialization allows people to learn their chosen tasks better, because they can concentrate, for example, on making very good paper-bag puppets rather than on trying to produce puppets and knitted goods as well. In this way, specialization increases the quality of products available to consumers. It is efficient, too, in that specialization allows for an increase in the quantity of goods and services available. In providing the service of a bank in Mini-Society, one citizen may peform all the tasks. She or he may act as teller, keeping records on transactions and being nice to customers, too. The citizen may also act as advertising director, creating ads and campaigns. He or she may keep the books balanced (act as accountant) and manage the bank's employees. However, what will happen to the banker who is an excellent accountant and ad manager but who cannot cope as well with employees and customers? What about the banker who has good math skills but poor social ones? And what about the banker who can perform all these tasks but not quickly enough to keep customers happy and the bank a growing concern? Specialization allows for an increase in the quantity of the goods and services by having people concentrate on their areas of expertise in cooperative ventures. In this way, working with others in a partnership situation may be a very positive experience.

So how do we make partnerships (specialization within a business) a viable alternative to working solo? One way is to clearly set forth the conditions and boundaries of the partnership before going into a business. Through a legal contract or gentlemen's agreement, many problems may be solved before they arise.

A gentlemen's agreement may or may not be legally binding in a society. Because the details are unwritten, they are difficult if not impossible to prove when a dispute arises. This type of agreement may be desirable because it shows good faith in the work of another, and it can be workable when dealing with persons of integrity. Students may wish to use the gentlemen's agreement (perhaps with a witness to the verbal agreement) to show this good faith, especially when dealing with a close friend. An old adage says that business and friendship don't mix. For some of your students, this may prove true.

A legal contract is a written agreement of the details of partnership that is legally binding, signed by both parties, and may include several elements (that also may be incorporated in a gentlemen's agreement). In a Mini-Society, articles of partnership may include the division and extent of ownership. The articles of partnership may detail the percentage of the business owned by each partner and may specify a particular business rather than including any spin-off businesses. In some instances, students may attempt to become "total" partners, sharing all profits to the extent of creating a communal buying effort as well as a business arrangement. This partnership generally calls for further specification of responsibilities and privileges and usually does not work well. An agreement concerning the division of labor within the business and a detailing of responsibility for certain aspects of the business may be included in the articles. Some forward-looking students also may include details on the dissolution of partnership, including how and when it may occur.

C. Activities

1. A class member can keep a journal of business disagreements. Then the teacher may present sample disagreements and elicit from the class possible solutions to the problems, e.g., making agreements or contracts before going into business.
2. The class can perform a socio-drama (role-playing situation) where two partners disagree. They will then reverse roles. Through this exercise, each student will better be able to understand the viewpoint of the other student.

3. Ask the students to answer the following questions:
    a. If you were in the banking business, what job would you choose to do?
    b. Who would you choose as your partner and why? (You can have more than one partner.)

    Using these questions, show how the responses of each student might differ for the following businesses: auction business, variety store, sports tutoring service, art products manufacturing business, class newspaper, bookkeeping service.
4. Have a career education specialist speak to the class on the skills necessary for a wide variety of jobs.
5. Make up a list of jobs in your Mini-Society. Have each student tell which one she or he would do best and which job she or he would do worst.

CHAPTER 12

CASE STUDIES /DEBRIEFINGS ON VALUES INQUIRY AND VALUES CLARIFICATION

I. Should We Charge for Everything?

A. **Objective**

After studying concepts in this section, students will be able to decide for themselves which activities warrant financial compensation and which are performed at zero price because people are members of a social system such as a family, a classroom, or a community.

B. **Clarification of Ideas and Principles**

A fear sometimes expressed by noninitiates in Mini-Society is that the students will become very mercenary and put a price tag on every action. This fear can be allayed and the possibility greatly lessened through the values-clarification debriefing discussed here.

Sometimes after being paid for their work in Mini-Society, students express the desire (or demand) to be paid for things outside the realm of traditional work roles. They may wish to be paid for matters that were previously considered matters of common courtesy or expected behavior (obligations as group members). It is possible that these ideas come from watching the adult society in operation. They have unknowingly internalized the concept that people are paid for work and their definition of work is anything they don't wish to do.

At this point in Mini-Society, the idea of nonpecuniary considerations should be discussed. Nonpecuniary is a term covering all costs, benefits, functions, and considerations that are not tied to money. This includes rights and responsibilities of individuals both to themselves and to their group. This discussion may require some digression into the nature of groups—the class, the family, the state, the nation, or even the Brownie or Cub Scout troop. It is important for the students to realize the benefits and costs of being a group member as well as the fact that they can willingly join some groups whereas they are born or legally tied into other groups.

Another nonpecuniary consideration that should be examined is personal pleasure along with related elements of self-respect, respect for others, etc. Have the students consider the case of Chris (or some student with a similar experience in your classroom). Chris was working as a bank teller for a good salary; however, the bank owner yelled at her a lot and often paid her late. She quit the job and went to work for another employer for a great reduction in wages, but in her new job she received her wages on time and was spoken to kindly. Some of her friends believed this was a foolish move for Chris to make. They thought that the extra money was worth the bad working conditions. Some of her friends thought that Chris had indeed made a smart move. They agreed with her that being paid late and being yelled at was not worthwhile, even given the extra money she earned. This tradeoff between working conditions and pay is a matter of decision for the individual. People must decide for themselves at what point the two balance out. When does the kind word become worth giving up the increment in pay? This is the economic concept of marginal rate of substitution and can apply to any situation in which two desirable or undesirable elements are weighed against one another.

C. Activities

1. Have the class discuss the following case study in terms of the purposes for which students attend school and the rights and responsibilities that go with this opportunity:

    Two children were busily talking as the teacher was giving directions. When asked to be quiet, they replied, "How much will you pay us?" After receiving an angry response from the teacher, they wanted to know how this was different from being paid for producing wallets.

2. Have the students make a list of those things they would do for a friend at zero price versus those things for which they want to be paid. Discuss the results.

3. Have the students make a list of those things they do as members of a family versus those things for which they receive an allowance. Discuss the different lists.

4. Lead a discussion on types of nonpecuniary rewards.

II.   Is It Easier to Steal Than To Work?

A. Objectives

After studying concepts in this section, students will be able to:

1. Identify four ways of obtaining income, such as earning, stealing, borrowing, and having it given to them.

2. Identify the problems and benefits of each way of obtaining income.

B. Clarification of Ideas and Principles

In many homes and classrooms, the expressed sentiment that it is easier to get money through stealing than through working would be met with severe disapproval if not out-and-out punishment. In Mini-Society, it is important to examine carefully these attitudes with the students, whether or not the actual phrase is voiced. Similar attitudes that occur and should be examined are that it is easier to borrow than to work and that it is easier to be given money than to work for it. Try to guide the discussion of these topics, but allow the students to weigh their own opinions and the costs and benefits of these in coming to conclusions.

Very young children do not understand the concept of property rights. This concept and its position in our society becomes internalized only through socialization. Help your students examine the concept by discussing the various ways to obtain money. People can work for money, borrow money from someone who worked for it, be given money as a gift from someone who worked for it, or steal money from someone who worked for it. The factor that all these have in common is that someone along the line worked for the money. When students begin to express their opinions on which way of obtaining money is the "best," remember that most of them come from backgrounds in which someone else (usually parents) earns money that transfers to the children as gifts. When the students discuss the advantages and disadvantages of each method, try to help them with logic rather than setting up arguments that easily can be knocked down. For example, one advantage of earning one's own money is the self-respect and self-sufficiency that can accompany the act. However, a very real disadvantage is that working for money takes up time that might be used in ways more pleasurable for the individual; an opportunity cost is involved. An advantage to borrowing money is that one can use the time that might have been spent in working to do other things. The disadvantage is that loans have to be paid back at some time, often with interest. This may mean that the borrower may eventually have to work longer and/or harder to repay the loan than if he or she had worked for the money to begin with. The advantage of a gift of money is twofold. The money needn't be repaid, and the time saved can also be used in other ways. However, there is often a nonpecuniary debt incurred as a result of a gift. The giver may not expect the money back, but she or he may expect certain behavior in return for her or his kindness. In other words, gifts sometimes come with strings attached. The advantage to stealing money is that one has the use of the money and time without the necessity of paying the money back. The disadvantage can be loss of self-respect and sometimes legal punishment if the thief is caught.

Be sure to discuss with the students what method of obtaining money they think is fair—both to themselves and to other people. Indicate that various societies have different values about these methods. Discuss what is considered proper in our society and what actually happens in practice. Try not to be too harsh on children if they lack a "work ethic" you consider important.

C. **Activities**
1. If and when a stealing incident occurs, elicit from the class during a group discussion different ways of getting income in their Mini-Society (a friend can give you money; you can work for money; you can borrow money from the bank, a friend, or a loan company; or you can steal money).
2. Role-play each of the ways of getting income. Emphasize pride in earning. Discuss the anger, guilt, and fear involved with stealing.
3. Have students write essays about stealing. Elements involved might be how the robbed person feels, how stealing affects their society, and the influence of TV programs on stealing.
4. Discuss ways to end stealing, such as whether punishment is a deterrent.
5. Discuss how it feels to earn money as compared to receiving it as a gift.

III. Fringe Benefits (Is Graft a Way Employers Pay for What They Want?)

A. **Objectives**
After studying concepts in this section, students will be able to:
1. Define *graft* and differentiate between graft payments and legal casting of dollar votes.
2. Present arguments to support their positions on the issue of whether graft serves a legitimate function.

B. **Ethical Dilemma**
In the fifth-grade Mini-Society country of Surf City, great commotion arose in a debriefing session. Class auction signs-ups were taken on a first-come, first-served basis, with six auctioning spaces available per week. Lee, the civil servant in charge of taking auction sign-ups and keeping auction records, had allegedly accepted a payoff from a classmate who wanted to sign up late for the first space on an already full slate. As the

debate over propriety progressed, some students expressed sympathy for Lee's position and for the position of Charles, who had made the payoff. Others called it bribery and condemned it. Those expressing sympathy claimed that it was just like buying anything else—you simply pay the person who can "deliver the goods" (the goods in this case being space on the auction slate). In his own defense, Charles wanted to know why paying Lee for the spot was any different from paying Peggy for a crocheted coin purse or paying a business consultant for advice. Those who opposed the action as improper claimed that it was different from the normal casting of dollar votes because it was breaking the rules already established for auction sign-ups. They compared the boys' action to the purchase of illegal goods.

The same type of incident can occur in Mini-Society if an employee pilfers materials from a business or if a worker embezzles funds. The justification usually presented in such cases is that wise employers expect such actions and make their budgets according to expected losses and that the extra materials or money are simply a form of salary that employers expect to pay in getting what they want.

C. Activities

1. Announce to the class at the beginning of a Mini-Society period that you will be selling three two-color pens during the next session of Mini-Society. (It could be anything you know has class appeal.) When you begin your debriefing session, announce to the class that the two-color pens will not be available because three students have already paid you for the right to buy the pens during the next session. Explain that this is a payoff and that it is receiving payment of dollars for goods and/or services. Advise the class that you found three more pens and that you will sell each to the highest bidder. Ask the students to differentiate between the two situations. (Legal and illegal casting of dollar votes.)

2. Ask the students if they can think of any situations where graft would be acceptable and why.

3. Have the students decide if graft should or should not be part of their Mini-Society and why.

4. Challenge the students to come up with a definition of graft as it pertains to their Mini-Society.

IV. Possession is Nine-Tenths of Something! (Does a Mini-Society Banker Have the Right to Spend Deposits?)

A. Objectives

After studying concepts in this section, students will be able to:

1. Explain why money deposited in a bank (either in the form of demand deposits or time deposits) belongs not to the banker but to the depositor.

2. Explain how a bank that has only demand deposits and time deposits can make a profit.

B. Ethical Dilemma

Janet was distraught. Six people were lined up at her bank demanding that she return money they had deposited. Unfortunately she did not have the 520 bionics she would need to pay them back. Janet asked the teacher if the subject could be discussed in the debriefing session that day in the third-grade Mini-Society, the Land of Bionic Children.

In the session, Janet told the class that she couldn't understand why depositors at her bank were angry. When the bank opened just two weeks ago, lots of people had been happy to put their money in the bank. Why, they'd given the money right to Janet, and she gave them in return a little book in which to write down the amount of money. Now they wanted the money back! Janet went on to explain that she had become a banker so she could make money, just like Tim had gone into the physical fitness lesson business to make money. When Andy, Patti, Paul, and others had put money into her bank, she had so much money that she decided to use some of it to buy wallets and cookies. There were loud protests from her depositors. "We put our money in your bank to keep it safe!" said Louise. "I put my money in there so I could write checks when I want to buy something," added Fred, "so the money still belongs to us!" Judy suggested that Janet sell the things she had bought in order to pay back her depositors. "I guess I *could* sell the wallets, but I ate the cookies a long time ago," Janet replied. Besides, she reasoned, the other kids had *given* her their money, so why couldn't she spend some of it? "I don't understand why people would want to be bankers if they couldn't spend some of the money," she said.

The idea of a bank in the classroom is enticing to many Mini-Society citizens, but the internal operations of a bank mystify them. Mini-Society bankers sometimes experience confusion concerning the difference between their own money and money held in trust for depositors. The confusion is generally more intense in younger citizens, but older students have misunderstandings as well. Even students who realize that bankers may make a profit by loaning out or investing a portion of the money from time and demand deposits sometimes have difficulty in determining a "safe" amount to keep in reserve to cover checks and withdrawals.

C. **Activities**
1. Discuss the role of a supermarket or movie theatre cashier. Emphasize to the class that the cashier collects money, but the money does not belong to that person. The cashier is paid a salary for performing a job. Compare these services to those provided by a bank.
2. Have the students bring in ingredients to make cookies in class. Tell the class to prepare the cookies, but you assume the responsibility for baking them. Later, inform the class that you gave the baked cookies to the other teachers. Discuss why this was unacceptable (e.g., just because something is in your possession doesn't mean you can use it at will).
3. Discuss the job of mail carriers, noting all the packages and letters they deliver but do not own. Compare the mail carrier to the banker, and discuss similarities.
4. Have a banker come to your class, or, if possible, take a field trip to a bank to observe the operations. Ask the banker to explain how banks make money or obtain information on bank loans, time deposits, and charges for services.

V. What Do You Mean, You're Broke? (Should Mini-Society Citizens Have the Right to Declare Bankruptcy?)

A. **Objectives**
After studying concepts in this section, students will be able to:
1. Define bankruptcy as a situation in which an individual is unable to pay his or her debts or a situation in which a court of law rules an individual (or a firm) insolvent and divides the liquidated assets among the creditors.
2. Establish their own positions on the issue of whether Mini-Society citizens should have the right to declare bankruptcy, and substantiate their positions using evidence and logic.

B. Ethical Dilemma

When Marty first got the idea to open his business, he was very excited. He decided to call it Marty's Wallet Factory. Although he did not have much money saved, Marty thought he had a wonderful way to begin without taking a loan from the bank. He would first buy all the materials and other things he needed to start his business. He would promise to pay for the materials and other items later, after he had a big profit from selling his first batch of wallets. He also promised to pay the salaries of his two employees, Larry and Helen, after some of the wallets had been sold. Marty and his workers began in earnest to produce wallets, which were dynamite-looking. Marty was so confident about making lots of money by selling his attractive wallets that he gave himself a special treat—he went on a little buying spree, purchasing some baseball cards from George, a cookie from Ted's Snack Shoppe, and even a necklace for his mother from Linda's Jewelry Store.

The first day Marty opened his wallet shop for business, he sold less wallets that he had anticipated. He kept selling a few wallets each day, but the trouble was that there were already two other wallet manufacturers in the class, and Marty had to sell his wallets for several quets per wallet less than he originally had planned to charge. By the end of the first week of business, all the people to whom Marty owed money were beginning to form themselves into an angry mob. Sensing trouble, Ms. Anthony began a debriefing session to discuss the problems encountered by Marty. Marty moaned that he was very confused about what to do. Even though he had sold all the wallets, he was able to pay only a few of his personal and business debts. Larry and Helen refused to help him produce more wallets unless they were paid for the time they had already worked. The owners of firms that had sold Marty the materials with which to make the wallets were demanding immediate payment. Help! Couldn't someone think of a solution for him?

The entire sixth-grade class listened to Bruce tell them about a television show about eighteenth-century England he had watched the night before. "And when people couldn't pay money they owed," concluded Bruce, "they threw them in debtor's prison." Some of the citizens vigorously applauded this as the solution for Marty, among them Marty's creditors. But Elizabeth, to whom Marty also owed quite a sum, disagreed. What good would it do to put Marty in jail? He wouldn't be able to pay back any of the money that way because he wouldn't be able to earn anything if he were imprisoned. Larry felt that if Marty were punished by some form of imprisonment, his creditors would at least have the satisfaction of seeing him unable to participate in Mini-Society.

Ms. Anthony chose this point at which to reenter the discussion. She suggested that the students may have gotten carried away with thoughts of punishment. She encouraged Alice, whose mother practiced business law, to speak out further when Alice mentioned the term *bankruptcy*. Alice explained that the judges of the court in Mini-Society might take over Marty's Wallet Factory; sell off anything left such as the felt scraps, thread, cash box, etc.; and divide the money from that sale among those to whom Marty owed debts. Even though his creditors probably wouldn't receive the full amount of Marty's debts, they at least would get some money. Then the slate would be wiped clean, and Marty could try to start anew, having learned a lesson about money management. "But that's not fair," Elizabeth claimed. She suggested that the court action was a good start but that Marty ought to be forced to pay off all of the debts *entirely*, perhaps by working without pay for those to whom he owed money. As the class resumed the problem-solving discussion, George muttered, "I'll sure be careful about whom I let buy on credit from now on!"

Does a declaration of bankruptcy and the process that follows result in the fair treatment of creditors and debtors? Under what, if any, circumstances should bankruptcy proceedings nullify the outstanding debts of a Mini-Society citizen? Should there be a separation of personal and business assets and liabilities when bankruptcy is declared? These are among the thought-provoking questions that can be considered when a Mini-Society citizen declares she or he is unable to pay a debt.

C. **Activities**
1. Borrow some Mini-Society money from several students, promising to pay each person back on a specified date. (You may tell each that the funds are to be used to go into some business.) With the students' money, buy goods and services during Mini-Society, making sure to spend all the money. On the due date, inform the students that you don't have the funds to pay them back, but that several options are available to rectify the situation: declare bankruptcy, work to pay off the debt, or sell whatever assets are available. Discuss the alternatives.
2. Ask a specialist (attorney) to visit your class to discuss the meaning of bankruptcy and the ramifications of declaring bankruptcy.
3. Ask students to define in their own terms what bankruptcy is, and ask them to think about how they would resolve a bankruptcy situation, providing reasons for the decision. Present possible resolutions to the class, and have students decide what course of action to take.

VI. . . . Good Intentions (Should Welfare Be Part of Mini-Society? If So, What Form Should It Take?)

A. **Objectives**
After studying concepts in this section, students will be able to:
1. Define *welfare* as tax-financed payments to certain individuals, which allows them purchasing power they would not otherwise have.
2. Establish their own positions for or against a welfare system in Mini-Society, and substantiate their positions using evidence and logic.

B. **Ethical Dilemma**
Ayn had gone bankrupt four times previously in Mini-Society, but never before had her bankruptcy left her so very deflated. She had no more places to go for business capital, and she had no ideas for a new business venture. Everyone in the class knew that her bankruptcies had not occurred for lack of energy on her part—she had really tried to make a go of all the businesses. The failures had been due to various factors such as drastic increases in production costs, unavailability of materials, and the competition of inexpensive and desirable products. In the same class was another citizen with a money problem. Jeff was new to the school, and he liked the idea of Mini-Society very much; there had been no Mini-Society at his other school. But because he was new to the class, Jeff had no Mini-Society money. Candyland had been in operation for quite some time, and most of the citizens had been in business or had salaried jobs for many weeks, so they had lots of money with which to start new businesses and purchase great products and services. Jeff had to find a way to get some money fast, or he wouldn't be able to join in all the activities going on in his new class. He figured it would take him some time to accumulate enough money to participate in the buying and, maybe, to start his own business.

That day in the debriefing session, Cynthia called attention to the fact that some classmates were experiencing difficulties. She explained that at one point her mother didn't have a job and their family had almost no money, "so we went on welfare until Mom could find a new job and make some money." Cynthia suggested that there could be welfare in the Mini-Society class for people who lost their jobs, went out of business, or had no money. "But how would we know who should get welfare?" questioned Terry. "And where would the money come from?" asked Alice. Cynthia explained that when her family was on welfare, the money had come from the government, so she reasoned "we could just take the welfare money out of the treasury." Joe was a step ahead of Cynthia and interrupted to tell the class that taking the money out of the treasury would mean that they would all be paying for the welfare payments when they had to pay their income taxes. "Besides that, wouldn't people go out of business or lose their jobs on purpose so they could get money without working?" asked Renee.

Similar debates are conducted in most Mini-Society classes at some time in the society's operation. The solutions vary greatly and include the retention of original infusion payments as a kind of guaranteed annual income, the imposition of a special income tax to support welfare payments, and the expressed stipulation of no welfare system. For Mini-Society students, the issue of whether to create a welfare system, and if so what type of system to create, can be a valuable and interesting learning experience.

C. Activities
1. During debriefing session, discuss the meaning of *welfare*.
2. Have a simulation in which students with *x* amount of Mini-Society money are taxed *x* percent, and then give that money to students who do not have money. Discuss the economic ramifications of this redistribution (effect on prices, buying power) as well as the social ramifications (everyone is taken care of; a way for students new to Mini-Society to become involved).
3. Vote on whether to install a welfare system and on what things would be designated under the category of welfare.
4. Allow the class to vote on whether they believe it would be fair to gather all the Mini-Society currency every three weeks and divide it equally among members of the class. What would be the ramifications of such a policy?

VII. He's Got More Than I've Got! (Should the Citizens of a Mini-Society All Have Equal Income?)

A. Objectives
After studying concepts in this section, students will be able to:
1. Explain arguments in favor of and against an egalitarian mechanism for allocating scarce resources.
2. Compare a market solution to a communalistic solution for distributing income among citizens.

B. Ethical Dilemma
Mini-Society had been in operation about five weeks when Brad spoke up in the debriefing session. "Why don't we take all the money in Millerville and give everybody an equal amount?" he asked. That way, Brad reasoned, no one would be rich and no one would be poor. The teacher determined how many millerbills there were in all of Millerville and put that number on the board. Class members helped do the arithmetic, dividing the total amount of money by the number of citizens who "resided' in the class/ country. In this way, they determined how much each of them would get if Brad's proposal were accepted: 340 millerbills. The teacher expected that anyone who had fewer than 340 millerbills would vote for the proposal and that anyone with more money would vote against the measure. When the topic was opened for discussion, the citizens were divided, but not along the lines the teacher had expected. Christine spoke up

against the proposal, even though she had only forty millerbills at the time. "I might get a really good business idea tomorrow or the next day. I want the chance to make lots of money if I get a good idea, and I want to do it myself!" Lisa, with 500 millerbills, agreed with Brad. She said that it was better to be sure you would have *some* money rather than taking the chance of having lots or of having very little. Peter pointed out that if Millerville's wealth were redistributed, they would have to redivide the money constantly or "in a week the same people who are rich now will be rich again, and the same ones who are poor would be poor."

The proposal to redistribute the wealth of a Mini-Society along egalitarian lines presents a theme, variations of which can occur at the beginning or at any point in the operation of a Mini-Society.

C. **Activities**
1. During a debriefing session, announce that all students will receive grades of "B" for all subjects listed on their final report cards. Discuss the advantages for some students (those doing less than "B" work) and the disadvantages to others (those doing "A" work). Discuss the problems that may arise as a result of this situation.
2. Take a survey to see how many students would remain in their current jobs if the amount of money they were able to receive were equal to the average amount they currently earn. Discuss the results.

VIII. Do-Gooders vs. Doers of Good (Should Mini-Society Citizens Report Other Citizens for Infractions of Rules?)

A. **Objectives**
After studying concepts in this section, students will be able to:
1. Differentiate between violations of law and violations of ethics.
2. Differentiate among crimes against society, crimes against individuals, and victimless crimes.
3. Establish their own positions concerning Mini-Society citizens reporting others for infractions of rules, and substantiate their positions using logic and evidence.

B. **Ethical Dilemma**
"Tattletale" is a familiar epithet in the world of elementary school children. It can be hurled with varying degrees of hostility and conviction, but the connotation invariably is negative. The accusation "tattletale" signaled the onset of a societal dilemma in the country of Economyville. Several citizens were using the debriefing sessions as opportunities to report other citizens' activities that they considered illegal or incorrect. One day Larry reported that Doug's business records weren't being kept properly. Mr. Green and many other citizens were concerned that bad feelings were starting to develop among the citizens and brought up the matter in the debriefing session.

Molly started the discussion by asking the group the question "Is telling on somebody like telling your mother that your little brother is playing with matches?" The question initiated a rather broad discussion in which there was much disagreement. Students referred to some of the situations they had witnessed on television programs to give examples substantiating their opinions. "On one program they call people who tell on others 'snitches.' They aren't good people at all. They turn in their friends, and the friends go to jail or get punished," one student said. "But on another show the guys who tell Tony things like that are good guys," replied another.

One group of students maintained that the propriety of reporting other citizens for breaking rules depended on whether the action of the errant citizen was hurting anyone else. For example, it would be improper for Larry to report Doug if the incorrectly kept records would only cause Doug problems later when he tried to straighten out his business books. But it would be proper to report Doug if he were purposely keeping business transactions off his records in order to avoid paying income taxes. Alicia, whose mother was an accountant, informed the group that in the United States people get money rewards for turning in people who have cheated on their taxes. Another group of citizens was firm in the opinion that it was *never* right to tell on others, and still another group said it was a citizen's *duty* to report anyone who was doing anything wrong. Carl straddled the fence when he maintained that it depends on the situation as to whether it is right to turn other people in. He convinced quite a few of his classmates when he explained that sometimes not everyone agrees that a certain way of doing things is wrong. "When everybody in a country thinks that it's wrong to do a certain thing, they should make it against the law. Then it's O.K. to report a person who breaks the law. But if only some people think it's wrong, then it's what my church calls 'a matter of conscience.'"

   The dilemma of whether and when to report a classmate for infraction of rules is one that may trouble students at any grade level. Mini-Society provides the opportunity for some frank and valuable soul searching in an open forum. In adult life, such ethical lines are drawn by each person, often for each new situation. A discussion of the subject at hand can serve to vividly illustrate to Mini-Society citizens that life contains many instances in which the "right" answer is difficult to ascertain.

C. **Activities**
   1. Establish a learning center that students can visit during Mini-Society period. Equip the center with short (one-paragraph), typed descriptions of situations in which students must decide what kind of crime has been committed: a crime against society (criminal); a crime against an individual (civil), or a victimless crime. Ask students to provide possible ways of dealing with the perpetrator. Collect the students' solutions, and discuss in a debriefing session their appropriateness and practicability.

      You could also use newspaper and/or magazine examples and have students discuss how they might resolve the situations presented.
   2. During a debriefing session, use the *Vehicle Drivers' Codebook* to discuss the difference between violators of laws and violators of ethics.
      a. Read some of the laws in the codebook, and have the class decide if the laws are fair and why they should be enforced.
      b. Provide the students with some examples that reflect proper ethics (courteous driving). Ask the students if and why these are just as important as the other laws.
   3. Establish a set of classroom/Mini-Society rules, or reappraise already existing rules. Are these rules of ethics, and why have they been established? Ask the students if they wish to alter any of the rules and why.

IX. Copycat, You Dirty Rat! (Should a Person Be Allowed To Protect Her or His Idea for a Business Venture?)

A. **Objectives**
   After studying concepts in this section, students will be able to:
   1. Explain the rationale for copyright and patent laws.
   2. Present arguments in favor of and against the appropriateness of patent and

copyright laws for their Mini-Society country.

3. Take a stand in favor of or against patent and copyright laws, and substantiate their views using logic and evidence.

B. Ethical Dilemma

After about three weeks of Mini-Society, business activity in the fourth-grade country of Bionic Kids was booming. There were numerous alternatives for spending money. Sara had just opened a business selling lovely necklaces with star designs that she had created herself. The very next day, though, Jenny began to sell necklaces, too. The problem was that the designs on Jenny's necklaces were almost identical to those that Sara had created. Sara began a vehement protest against the "theft" of her designs. The teacher took the opportunity to speak about competition versus monopoly in the debriefing session, but the controversy continued, centering around whether Sara had any legal or moral rights to the sole use of her designs. The teacher tried to explain the copyright and patent laws in the adult world but said that these might be very difficult to uphold in a Mini-Society, because a minor change in wording or technical design was legal even in the adult world. Some of the citizens thought that they ought to have sole right to the use of any designs or products they invented for at least a week and maybe for more than a week. Others thought that sole use should be theirs throughout the Mini-Society's existence. Still others were proponents of absolute competition; that is, anyone could use any idea no matter who originated it.

C. Activities

1. During a debriefing session, obtain copies of copyright and patent laws. Have a specialist (an attorney or employee of a patent office) visit the classroom and discuss the law.
2. If time permits, have students individually or collectively design or write something, and try to get a patent or copyright for it.
3. Role-play the situation of an inventor confronting someone who has marketed his or her invention without the inventor's consent.
4. Establish an art activity center (the art project should be unrelated to Mini-Society), making sure to include a few sample art designs. After the students have completed their own designs, collect them and compare them to the samples, then discuss the results.
5. Ask students to decide individually whether they are in favor of or against patent and copyright laws, and have them give at least one reason for their decisions.
6. Have the class collectively decide whether patent and copyright laws should be established for their Mini-Society.

X.   The Bunny Plop (Public Goods: Is Everybody's Business Nobody's Business?)

A. Objectives

After studying concepts in this section, students will be able to:
1. Define a public good as something belonging to the citizenry at large for the benefit of all.
2. Establish their own positions regarding responsibility for the maintenance of public goods, and substantiate their positions using logic and evidence.

B. Ethical Dilemma

When Ms. Adams first brought Hector to live in her classroom, everyone was delighted. Even though he was only a rabbit, the citizens of Star Land made him an honorary Mini-Society citizen. Ms. Adams had made it clear that Hector was going to belong to all of them. They would all have the fun of watching him and studying him, but they would all have to share in the responsibility of feeding him and cleaning his cage. "Fine," they all had agreed. At first everyone wanted to feed Hector, but after a week passed, it was time for a less pleasant job. *Someone* had to clean Hector's cage! *No one* volunteered. Ms. Adams was about to do the job herself. After all, just because the students didn't want to do the job was no reason to make Hector suffer with a dirty cage. That day Ms. Adams brought up the matter of Hector's cage in the Mini-Society debriefing session. She explained that because Hector belonged to them all, they were all responsible for his care. "Sure," they all agreed again. Several students testified that they had volunteered all week to feed the rabbit. "But now he must have his cage cleaned, and no one is willing to do that, and we must deal with this," explained the teacher.

It was suggested then that if no one wanted to volunteer to do the job, maybe the Mini-Society treasury should *pay* someone to do it. Of course, the students realized that paying someone from the treasury would make the care of Hector a civil service job, paid with their tax dollars. They also acknowledged that the pay might have to be relatively high, because the citizens seemed to find any cleanup job a distasteful one. Lisa drew an analogy from the real world. She explained that her uncle worked in a public park in the neighborhood cutting the grass, caring for the trees, and doing general cleanup. "The park belongs to all of us, but we don't all go there after school or after work to take care of it. We just pay my uncle and other people to do it for us."

Many of the students agreed that paying for Hector's care out of tax dollars was a proper thing to do. But one young citizen drew another analogy to the adult world, which prolonged and extended the discussion. Jim compared Hector's care to the support of educational television stations. He informed the class that these channels were sometimes called public television stations and that anyone with a TV could turn it on and watch the programs for free. Because the stations had no advertisements, they weren't supported by businesses through payment for commercials; someone just came on the air every once in a while and asked the people watching to send in some money. "But you don't *have* to do it," explained Jim. Some of the students began to question whether they should take money out of their taxes to pay for Hector's care. Perhaps the payment for the rabbit's care should come from donations (of both money and time) from people who *wanted* to participate. The students went on to discuss the matter for some time before coming to a solution appropriate for their Mini-Society.

Many Mini-Society countries experience some controversy over the maintenance of public goods. Although citizens almost universally are willing to accept the right or privilege of enjoying a public good, many are unwilling to accept accompanying responsibilities. In a discussion of the benefits and costs of public goods, be prepared to hear some disagreement among Mini-Society citizens about whether the costs should be borne by all through a mandate.

C. **Activities**
    1. During a debriefing session, discuss what is meant by a public good. Ask the students to give examples of public goods they have encountered in their day-to-day experiences (at home, school, park, etc.).
    2. Start a garden in your classroom. Discuss the benefits and liabilities of caring for the garden. What will be the results if the garden does not receive care?
    3. Announce to the class that they will be shown a special film you know they will enjoy. On the day of the movie, make sure that something on the projector is not working properly. Tell the class you're sorry that it will be impossible to show the movie, because the projector is broken. Ask the class to resolve how the projector (a public

good) might be cared for so that other classrooms would not have to experience the same disappointment.

4. Arrange to go to the school library for a reading period. Go in before the class arrives and scatter books throughout the library so that when your students arrive they will find the library messy. Tell the students that before they can use the library facilities, they must help straighten it up. During a debriefing session, ask the students who should assume the responsibility for the care of the library (a public good) and how the problem of the messy library might be resolved.

5. Ask the students to decide how they intend to care for public goods in their classroom, making sure that each student gives a reason substantiating his or her position.

XI. The Benevolent Dictator (Do Teachers or Other Authority Figures Have the Right To Set Themselves Up as the Government in Their Classroom Mini-Societies?)

A. Objectives

After studying concepts in this section, students will be able to:

1. Define and differentiate among a dictatorship, republic, and democracy.
2. Express their personal preferences for a specific form of government in Mini-Society and state reasons for their choices.
3. Differentiate between a parliamentary and presidential form of government. (Optional)

B. Ethical Dilemma

It was a big day in the sovereign state of Hyper-Society. The citizens were holding a revolution, which had been scheduled the previous day with the teacher's permission. Though they were very fond of their teacher, students in the Mini-Society country were distressed by her usurping power from their government officials until she had de facto become the Mini-Society government. The revolutionary action was the culmination of a long chain of events that led the students to question seriously the right of their teacher to unilaterally impose regulations in a society that presumably was a republic.

In the past weeks, Mrs. Claybark had taken several actions that the students considered dictatorial. For example, she had imposed a noise pollution tax on citizens whose business activities became "too boisterous." No vote was taken on the tax imposition. The acceptable noise level, determined solely by the teacher, varied from day to day according to her mood. In another instance, Mrs. Claybark had intervened at the class auction when one citizen had bid more hypocents for an item than he possessed. She ordered that the citizen *must* buy the item for the amount bid, even if he had to borrow hypocents in order to do so. In addition, she levied a fine of twenty hypocents on the citizen for having overbid. Finally, the students had taken the problem home to their parents, enlisting their aid. Though the students expected no repercussions in other areas of the school curriculum as a result of the anticipated revolution, they elicited promises from their parents to help protect student rights should the teacher take unexpected offense at the political action.

"Mrs. Claybark, when Mini-Society started you said that it was going to be *our* country and that we would all be equal citizens. But you're not acting that way," the citizens began. The coup d'etat they conducted was, indeed, quite polite. They argued that the teacher had no right to set herself up as their government during Mini-Society. They cited examples of her encroaching dictatorial policies. In her own defense, the teacher argued that the students were too young and immature to act completely as their own government—there were so many things they could not do and decisions they could not make for themselves. She did finally relinquish control to them, however, and they eventually set up a modified parliamentary system. Mrs. Claybark became an elected official in the government, but the students maintained safeguards against any official usurping power from the citizens.

Similar situations occur in many Mini-Societies. Teachers or dictatorial students often usurp some degree of governmental power supposedly residing with elected officials or with the citizenry at large. Sometimes this takes the form of overt action and in other instances comes about through covert manipulation of citizens' decisions. Actual revolutions have been relatively rare in Mini-Societies, although in some classrooms the citizens become sufficiently distressed to speak up concerning the teacher's intervention in their government. More often, students merely suffer in silence. By overtly usurping power or covertly manipulating the governance of a society, an authority figure may be reinforcing the students' suspicions that Mini-Society will not truly allow them to make their own decisions and bear consequences. In still other classroom situations, the students are not distresssed at all by an authority's assumption of governmental power.

C. Activities

1. Initiate class discussion by introducing the terms *dictatorship, republic,* and *democracy*. Ask for definitions and then amplify them, if necessary, keeping the meaning simple.

   Dictatorship— is a government in which one person makes the decisions for the society; that person has absolute power.

   Republic— is a government in which a leader is usually a president, but the power to make decisions is controlled by elected officials.

   Democracy— is a government in which the power to make decisions is held directly by the people in their society.

2. Relate the dictatorial experience that preceded this lesson, and ask the students what form of government this represents and why.

3. You might want to make up some additional situations to clarify the students' understanding of the concepts. Ask the students how each situation might be handled under the other forms of government.

4. Introduce a situation familiar to the students which calls for a decision (e.g., How do we decide what games to play at recess?). Ask for solutions based on a democracy, a republic, and a dictatorship.

5. Divide the class into groups of three to four students, and:
   a. Have each group role-play one situation and demonstrate how it would be resolved under a dictatorship, a republic, and a democratic form of government.
   b. Have nonparticipants critique the role playing for authenticity.

6. Have students specify, in writing, which form of government they each prefer and why.

7. Spend one day of Mini-Society as a dictatorship, one day as a republic, and one day as a democracy. Discuss the positive and negative features.

XII. **Appetizers, Entrees, and Desserts! Is Mini-Society Just a Dessert? (Should Students Be Fined Mini-Society Money for Infractions of School Rules?)**

A. **Objectives**

After studying concepts in this section, students will be able to:

1. Differentiate between academic school subjects and recreational activities that are sometimes included in the school day.
2. Categorize Mini-Society as either an academic learning experience or a recreational activity and substantiate the categorization using evidence and logic.

B. **Ethical Dilemma**

Betty was not particularly interested in her arithmetic lessons this semester. She was enjoying her reading group work as well as science lessons and art instruction, and she was really involved in learning economics in her classroom Mini-Society, Land of Dinosaurs. For several days now, Betty had neglected to do her assigned lessons in arithmetic until Mr. Singer approached her. He said he thought she had been spending too much time and effort on her Mini-Society business and not enough time on her multiplication problems, so he was going to exclude her from participation in Mini-Society for a couple of days. Betty protested and asked that the matter be discussed in the interaction–discussion group that day. Mr. Singer consented. Mr. Singer and Betty both explained the situation to the whole class in the debriefing session. Some of the citizens insisted that the action was unfair. "That would be like not letting people participate in science for not doing their language arts work," maintained many of the students. Someone then suggested that Betty be made to pay a fine of ten tyrannosaurus bills for not having completed the arithmetic lesson rather than having all Mini-Society participation taken away.

The citizens of the Land of Dinosaurs debated long and hard over this issue. In the course of the debate they discussed whether participation in various school activities was a right or a privilege. They also discussed the responsibilities that go along with both rights and privileges. Someone pointed out that fining a person Mini-Society money for breaking rules that had nothing to do with Mini-Society was treating it as a game instead of a school subject.

Teachers and students in many classes are tempted to treat Mini-Society as a recreational activity. Perhaps this is because the experience-based learning that takes place through Mini-Society is so very enjoyable. However, it is important that the issue of whether Mini-Society is a treat or an academic program be discussed with students and teachers alike. Through such a discussion, the group as a whole can determine to what extent Mini-Society is to be treated as a "just desert" or "just a dessert."

C. **Activities**

1. Initiate class discussion on why the right to participate in Mini-Society should be taken away from disruptive students. Ask students the following questions: (a) Would anybody suggest taking a math assignment away from disruptive students? Why or why not? (b) What are the differences between something academic and something recreational? (c) Can something academic be fun?
2. Have students individually list three things that are academic and three things that are recreational in their school day. Share the lists with the rest of the class to see if there is agreement.
3. As a class activity, go through subjects of the school day and decide what academic components are involved in each (reading, math, science), including Mini-Society.
4. As a follow-up activity, ask students to list as many academic activities as they can that are components of Mini-Society. Have the students include the ways in which the activity is academic. Do the same with recreational components of Mini-Society. Allow students to share and compare results.

PART V

SUMMARY AND REVIEW

CHAPTER 13

SUMMARY AND REVIEW

This chapter provides you with a review of the major principles of the Mini-Society instructional system. As you read it, you'll have the opportunity to go over some of the procedures that have been detailed in the preceding chapters as well as those ideas that you've begun to generate for your own class. The Mini-Society is an experience-based educational system predicated on the belief that individuals learn by doing. Mini-Society is comprised of two interwoven components: the experience, and the formal debriefing of the concepts and ideas derived from the experience. Correctly implemented, Mini-Society simultaneously gives students new information and concepts as well as a sense of personal capability—students become fully aware that they possess the capability to utilize or act upon their knowledge.

The whole Mini-Society learning process starts with the students' frustration over not having enough of something they want. Although all the students undoubtedly have experienced this frustration before, the situations often have gone unresolved, and anxiety and tension hang in the air. In their Mini-Society, the students will confront and assess the different ways of dealing with the basic, life-long economic problem of scarcity.

To generate the Mini-Society and increase students' coping and decision-making skills, you should *find a situation in which the students actually experience scarcity*— a situation in which their wants are greater than the resources available to satisfy these wants. For example, you may call attention to the "main attraction" learning center and the fact that not everyone is getting to spend the time there that they'd like. If you feel that there is not sufficient interest in any of the activities presently available in the classroom, you may create a scarcity situation by providing a number of highly motivating materials such as colorful plastic puzzles, art media, tape recorders and tapes, or manipulative games. When you have placed these in an accessible area, the students will soon find that the demand for the materials, or the time to use them, far exceeds the supply. Thus, in initiating the Mini-Society, you focus on and then observe the students' reactions to the fundamental concept of economics: the existence of scarcity.

As the students begin to express their unhappiness about not having enough of a particular item or activity, you should note the complaints but continue to bide your time. When about half the class has voiced dissatisfaction, call them together for discussion. The discussion or debriefing group plays a pivotal role in the Mini-Society, so it should generate the maximum amount of student interaction. You will probably find that this participatory interaction will develop naturally, because the problem solving that will be the focus of these debriefings arises out of the students' firsthand experiences in

Mini-Society. During these debriefings you will be presenting and discussing in technical terms the economic principles and information that the students have just experienced. You will also examine in these sessions the philosophical, political, and governmental value dilemmas that have arisen, and you will explore the various alternatives.

The main problem to be resolved during the first few discussions is how to determine who gets time with the scarce resources. You can be assured that the students themselves will bring up alternative solutions to the problem of how to divide up, distribute, ration, or allocate an activity they all find desirable. Using their own terminology, they will discuss the advantages and disadvantages of various allocative strategies such as the first-come, first-served method; a lottery or drawing; force; need; and price variation.

The class usually decides to be paid for activities or behaviors that all students believe they can accomplish (being on time for school, handing in homework, etc.). Your role in this process, and throughout most of Mini-Society, is facilitative; encourage and help students narrow their list to the basic activities that they agree all students could and should attempt. Their list should not be overwhelming or impossible to accomplish. Remember, the purpose of the list is to create a means of getting money into the system—*not* setting up behavior modification. A long list of behaviors inevitably results in an unproductive economy. Stress that everyone will receive a tangible reward for performing the agreed-upon behaviors, then introduce the idea that the reward will be an income that may be used to buy the time with the high-interest activity as well as in other ways.

The group will immediately grasp the relationship between receiving income for activities and being able to spend the money. Almost intuitively, the students will want to spend part of their incomes and keep part (for varying reasons). The value should be more than a single monetary unit per day, but be careful not to allow the group to set the value *too* high. A rate of between five and ten units of currency a day seems to work out well, because at this rate some students will accrue the maximum income and a few others will not. This variation in income among students works to reinforce the entrepreneurship that develops during the course of the Mini-Society.

With your assistance, the citizenry usually hires civil servants, called paymasters, to ascertain whether individuals have earned their payment. Citizens also hire a treasurer and money cutters. Because many students apply for these jobs, the citizens should develop job application forms and a method for interviewing the applicants. It is interesting to note that most students do achieve maximum income, as they live up to the pay standards they have set as a class.

The class will decide what to call the reward units. Whatever the decision—room 15 pandas, gleps, quets, framistrams, etc.—they will want some help in issuing the units. (Civil servants, however, will soon become responsible for the money supply.) These units become the society's currency and can be used in whatever transactions the group agrees upon.

For the first several days, the students should be paid immediately after their performance: pay Tuesday morning for Monday's fulfillment of responsibilities, Wednesday for Tuesday's, and so on. Like most of us, the Mini-Society citizens will begin to spend money as soon as they receive some income. The first use of the currency should be buying time with the high-interest activity, so that an immediately functioning reward system is established. As the system continues into the next week and the need for immediate gratification abates a weekly payday should be established.

After several days, the Mini-Society that has begun to evolve in your classroom may move in many different directions. Your students will develop a combination of experiences related to their society. You will find that, from this point on, the model becomes largely self-sustaining, and your role as teacher becomes primarily that of observing and extending learning opportunities inherent in the economic environment.

For many students, the Mini-Society provides their first conscious experience in making decisions and then bearing the consequences of those decisions. They are perplexed about how to spend their incomes—for learning centers? erasers? felt-tip pens? to rent space for business? to buy consulting time? Just making any decision can be a long ordeal. When one of your students who has just suffered this trauma finally makes a decision, whatever its quality, you should give the child a smile, a wink, or some other form of approval.

Once the society is established and in operation, you can use a variety of approaches to help students move ahead. One such approach is the auction, which becomes a keenly anticipated and valuable learning tool in Mini-Society. Prior to the auction itself, students should discuss the basics of auction decorum, lest it deteriorate into a shouting match that brings the principal to your room wondering if there's been a revolution. Bidding should be done by raising hands or bidder cards, and careful records of all transactions should be kept. Keep in mind the importance of scheduling the auctions on days when most students will have money with which to participate.

Another approach that facilitates Mini-Society activity is creating a learning center on how to start a business. As the citizens begin to discover the entrepreneurial opportunities provided by Mini-Society, they will want to know how they can become proprietors and what things they should consider in planning a business. Through a learning center, games, consultation, and the group debriefing sessions, students can explore the market survey as a method of assessing demand, the selection of a business location, start-up and maintenance costs, advertising, record keeping, and government regulations.

You will probably find that your own consulting services are much in demand from this time forward. As the youngsters try out their newly acquired knowledge in actual enterprises, they may find that they need even more understanding to make their businesses successful. They'll begin to question you about what should be done, and you can announce that your time may be purchased during Mini-Society and that you will act as a hired consulting agent for any firm seeking advice.

The opportunities also exist for you to bring in or let the students find outside consultants. Imaginative business ideas often can be generated from older students and parents. If there is a junior or senior high school in the vicinity, it may be a rich source of potential consultants. Parents can offer many consulting services—from teaching children saleable skills outside of school to lending (selling) their expertise during the Mini-Society period.

Classes will vary in their proclivities to create innovative businesses. Almost all classes will create banks, loan companies, insurance companies, wallet-making businesses, and a variety of ingenious services. The only limits to the range of activities are the children's imaginations. For example, one eight-year-old, a budding pianist, offered his services as a music teacher. Under the direction of an aide, the teacher allowed him to take his pupils to the music room (which had been rented from the principal), where he gave fifteen-minute piano lessons. Another student had her father teach her to use the family workshop so she could make small jewelry boxes; one child, with consultation from a craft-oriented parent, made papier-mâché sculptures to sell to classmates.

Along with the many small businesses that evolve from your students' desires to create or meet the demands of their classmates, you will almost certainly see the development of financial institutions and journalistic enterprises. Banks and/or loan companies generally appear first, the result of some students' not having enough money and wanting to borrow more and some students' having too much and not wanting to carry it around all the time. An insurance company may crop up after a theft or loss or following the return of the citizens who were absent on payday and missed their weekly compensation. Some form of stock market structure may develop as students solicit investors in their businesses, promising a share of the profits in return for a contribution. One or more of the students, seeing the need for increased communication and advertising, may use incipient writing and artistic skills to produce a newspaper.

Because almost all Mini-Society activities require the use of classroom or school space, the buying, selling and renting of real estate introduces the students to the concepts of property ownership and land value. Mortgage payments and rental agreements as well as what constitutes a desirable piece of property are given careful consideration.

The governmental structure of the Mini-Society will, like the private sector, reflect the values and concerns of the students. After the society has run for three to six weeks, the class may wish to initiate an income tax system or a sales tax in order to continue to pay income for the behaviors they had identified in the beginning. If such a tax structure is initiated, students will need to understand that, basically, the government provides them with certain services and that it is supported by those whom it serves through a tax system. Also, they should realize that payments for behaviors are, in essence, a guaranteed annual income and that they as a society must either bear the costs of such a decision or discontinue the payments.

The class will begin to see parallels to the tax system in the adult world and may wish to establish some allowable deductions and some nontaxable income categories. This experience usually leads to the formation of governing bodies that can rule on taxation and other legislative concerns. Taxation almost inevitably spurs the desire for representation. The creation of a representative body can also streamline the functioning of the society by relieving the entire discussion group of minor decisions. When you arrive at this stage in Mini-Society, you will see how effectively the process gives the students an understanding of governmental structure and a chance to try a participatory democracy.

The Mini-Society may continue for as long as you feel the class is deriving educational benefits. It may be done for a short period of time (ten weeks is the recommended minimum), or it may serve as the social studies focal point for an entire semester or year. Once the youngsters have grasped the relationship between the effort they expend and the rewards they can receive, they are often reluctant to let go of the system. This bears out the assumption upon which the Mini-Society instructional system is based: individuals learn concepts through real situations in which they play active roles, and they are highly motivated to follow through on those decisions in which they have taken part. The Mini-Society citizens are not playing a game. Their Mini-Society is very real to them—so real, in fact, that you will probably find them reluctant and sometimes even unwilling to exchange U.S. dollars for their own currencies.

PART VI
APPENDIXES

APPENDIX 1

Sample Scarcity Worksheet

(answers are printed in italics for teachers)

NAME _____

Circle the best answer.

1. Every person has (enough things, *unlimited wants*, too much).

2. Making things that people want means that we must use our (products, *resources*).

3. Circle the two most likely to be resources.

 trees    electricity    cake

4. There is only so much of every resource. All resources are limited. (*True*, False).

Fill in the blanks.

5. When people want more resources than there are, there is

    _____*(scarcity)*_____ .

6. The bigger the wants and the less the resources, the more

    _____*(scarcity)*_____ there is.

7. Name three ways to deal with the scarcity of ice cream. (*answers may vary*)

    _____

    _____

    _____

160

APPENDIX 2

How To Write a Check

Materials:

For this lesson you will need to duplicate blank checks for the students. You may want to laminate the large sample of a blank check to use for demonstration (you can wipe it clean after writing on it with a crayon), or you may use an overhead projector.

Look at the sample checks. Also included is a plan for producing checkbooks.

Procedure:

1. Each student should have several copies of blank checks for practice.

2. Complete one or two checks as a group. You can use the laminated sample as a demonstration model.

3. Have the students each write one of their friends a check for more practice.

Note: This lesson might also be presented as a math lesson, and the students can introduce checks into their society as they wish. A learning center might also be set up.

Lesson:

Each time you write a check, it is like taking money out of the bank and giving it to someone.

Your check has to tell all of the following information:

1. To whom you want to give the money.

Write the name of the person you want to give the check to here. It says, "Pay to the order of . . ."

Name_____ Check number _____
Address_____ Date _____ 19 ____
Bank number_____

Pay to the order of: _Mary Smith_____ $_____

_____ Rainbows

⊛BANK'S NAME signed_____

account number _____

2. How much you want to give this person.

   Write the amount of money here (use numbers first).

Name _____	Check number _____
Address _____	Date _____ 19 ___
	Bank number _____

Pay to the order of: _Mary Smith_ _____ $ _55.00_

_____ Rainbows

⊕ BANK'S NAME   signed _____

account number _____

3. Now use words instead of numbers to write the same amount of money.

   Write the words here.

Name _____	Check number _____
Address _____	Date _____ 19 ___
	Bank number _____

Pay to the order of: _Mary Smith_ _____ $ _55.00_

Fifty - five _____ Rainbows

⊕ BANK'S NAME   signed _____

account number _____

162

(Writing the number in words insures that the person to whom the check is written doesn't add a few numbers and make the amount larger. Also, it helps to make the amount clearly understood—especially if you write messy numbers. A line after the number in words also prevents a larger number from being added.)

4. Be sure to put the date on the check.

Name. *Bob Jones*
Address *Room 10*
Check number _____
Date *Oct 3* 19 *83*
Bank number_____

Pay to the order of: *Mary Smith* $ *55.00*
Fifty - five ———————— Rainbows
BANK'S NAME signed _____
account number _____

5. Write your name and address on the check.

6. You may want to write the check number, beginning with *1*.

Name. *Bob Jones*
Address *Room 10*
Check number *1*
Date *Oct 3* 19 *83*
Bank number_____

Pay to the order of: *Mary Smith* $ *55.00*
Fifty - five ———————— Rainbows
BANK'S NAME signed _____
account number _____

7. Finally, sign the check with your name.

Name _Bob Jones_	Check number _1_
Address _Room 10_	Date _Oct 3_ 19 _83_
	Bank number _____

Pay to the order of: _Mary Smith_ $ _55.00_

Fifty – five _____ Rainbows

BANK'S NAME signed _Bob Jones_

account number _____

Sample blank check for use in demonstration lesson on how to write a check. (This could be made larger and laminated.)

Name _____	Check number _____
Address _____	Date _____ 19 ___
	Bank number _____

Pay to the order of: _____ $ _____

_____ Rainbows

BANK'S NAME signed _____

account number _____

APPENDIX 3

Plan for Making Checkbooks

Sample plan for making checkbooks.

Staple several blank forms (checks and balance sheets) to a square of folded construction paper.

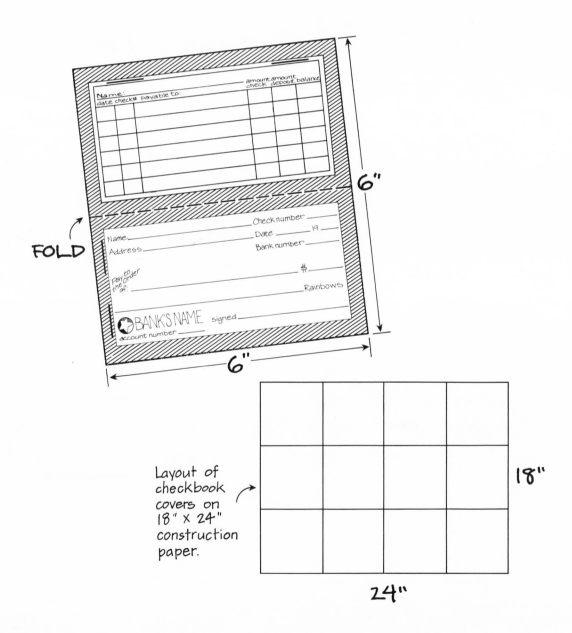

Layout of checkbook covers on 18" × 24" construction paper.

Sample blank forms for a checkbook:

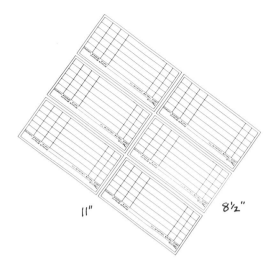

11"   8½"

Name_____ Check number_____

Address_____ Date_____ 19___

Pay to the order of: _____ Bank number_____

_____ $._____

_____ Rainbows

⊕ BANK'S NAME   signed_____

account number_____

	Name:			amount	amount	
date	check#	payable to:		check	deposit	balance

APPENDIX 4

How To Balance a Checkbook

Materials:

For this lesson you will need to duplicate blank balance sheets for the students. You may want to use the overhead projector or a large copy of the balance sheet for demonstration. Examples of how to construct a checkbook and sample sheets are included in the lesson on writing a check.

Procedure:

1. Each student will need at least one copy of a balance sheet.

2. Complete several transactions with the students. Do these in a series.

3. Give the students a new balance sheet, and then give them several problems. Check to see that the balance sheets are prepared properly. You may want to use checkbooks.

Lesson:

When you have a checking account at the bank, it is like having a certain amount of money on hand, because you can write a check for less than or equal to the amount you have in the bank. When the person who receives the check goes to the bank, the bank will give that person the amount of money indicated on the check; then your account will have that much less money in it.

Because every time you write a check it is like taking money out of your account, you have to keep a careful record of each check you write. You also must keep a careful record of money you put into your account.

(You may want to discuss a bounced check.)

Each time something happens (you make a transaction), use one line of the balance sheet.

Write the date under the column labeled *date*.

Write the check number under the column labeled *check*.

Record to whom you wrote the check. Write the person's name under the column labeled *payable to*.

Enter the amount of the check in the appropriate column, or, if you are making a deposit, write the amount of the deposit under its column heading.

Finally, write the balance at the end of the transaction. The balance is the sum of a deposit transaction, and the difference of a withdrawal or check written to remove money from the bank.

This is how you record transactions (do this series with the class):

First write your name on the balance sheet. Then let's say that you have deposited $100 in your account. Your beginning balance will be $100. If you deposited that money on October 11, your balance sheet would look like this.

Name: JACK				amount check	amount deposit	balance
date	check#	payable to:				
oct 11		DEPOSIT			100.00	100.00

Let's suppose that you wrote a check to the bakery when you bought a cake. The check was written on October 14. Write the date. The number of the check was #1 (the first check you wrote).

Name:		JACK		amount check	amount deposit	balance
date	check#	payable to:				
OCT 11		DEPOSIT			100.00	100.00
OCT 14	1	MARY'S BAKERY		8.00		

Write the name of the bakery on the same line. Now enter the amount of the check under the appropriate column. You paid $8 for the cake.

Now you have to write in your balance. Because you had $100 to start and you wrote a check to the bakery for $8, it is as if you took $8 out of your account to give to the bakery. Subtract the $8 from the $100 to get a balance of $92.

Name: JACK					
date	check#	payable to:	amount check	amount deposit	balance
OCT 11		DEPOSIT		100.00	100.00
OCT 14	1	MARY'S BAKERY	8.00		92.00

When you make a deposit, you add money to your balance. When you write a check, you subtract money from your balance.

Let's try another example. Suppose you wrote a check to Bill Smith for $54 on October 17. This was the second check you wrote. What would your balance sheet look like?

Name: JACK					
date	check#	payable to:	amount check	amount deposit	balance
OCT 11		DEPOSIT		100.00	100.00
OCT 14	1	MARY'S BAKERY	8.00		92.00
OCT 17	2	BILL SMITH	54.00		38.00

Next, you go to the bank and add or deposit $50 into your account. You do this on October 20. What does your balance sheet look like?

Name: JACK			amount check	amount deposit	balance
date	check#	payable to:			
OCT 11		DEPOSIT		100.00	100.00
OCT 14	1	MARY'S BAKERY	8.00		92.00
OCT 17	2	BILL SMITH	54.00		38.00
OCT 20		DEPOSIT		50.00	88.00

Every time you write a check or make a deposit, you should balance your checkbook. This insures that you won't write a check for money that is not in your account.

Balancing your checkbook is as easy as adding and subtracting, if you keep a careful record of each check and each deposit. The best time to do it is immediately after you have written a check or made a deposit.

Give your class several other examples. If they have constructed checkbooks, let them write checks out to their friends and then balance their checkbooks.

APPENDIX 5

How To Balance a Savings Account Book

Materials:

For this lesson you will need to duplicate blank balance sheets for the students. You may want to use an overhead projector to do a sample as a group of students follows along. Consult the following samples.

Procedure:

1. Each student will need several copies of blank balance sheets.

2. Complete several transactions in a series with the students.

3. Give the students several problems, and then check to see that their balance sheets are prepared properly.

Lesson:

After you deposit into or withdraw from your account, you will want to keep a record of it in your savings book.

Name the columns in your savings book.
1. Date
2. Deposit (+)
3. Withdrawal (−)
4. Interest (what the bank gives you periodically for keeping money with them)
5. Balance (the total left in the bank after each transaction)

Each time something happens (you make a transaction), use one line.

If you make a deposit, write the amount under the heading *deposit*, and withdrawals will go under the heading *withdrawal*.

Interest is the amount bankers give you for keeping money with them. Never subtract the interest from the balance. It is money the bank is giving you. You always add the interest.

Always write the date when something happens (you make a transaction).

The balance is the new amount after everything has taken place. It is the new total after you have added a deposit, subtracted a withdrawal, or added interest.

Sample lessons:

1. Susan deposits 200 rainbows into the bank on February 2. Her bank book looks like this:

Name SUSAN				
date	deposit	withdrawal	interest	BALANCE
Feb 2	200			200

2. On March 3, Susan made a deposit of 75 rainbows. Her bank book looks like this:

Name SUSAN				
date	deposit	withdrawal	interest	BALANCE
Feb 2	200			200
Mar 3	75			275

3. On March 6, Susan received 3 rainbows in interest. Now her bank book looks like this:

Name	SUSAN			
date	deposit	withdrawal	interest	BALANCE
Feb 2	200			200
Mar 3	75			275
Mar 6			3	278

4. On March 16, Susan needed some money. She withdrew 35 rainbows. Now her bank book looks like this:

Name	SUSAN			
date	deposit	withdrawal	interest	BALANCE
Feb 2	200			200
Mar 3	75			275
Mar 6			3	278
Mar 16		35		243

Sample blank balance sheet for savings account.

Name				
date	deposit	withdrawal	interest	BALANCE

layout on
8½ × 11"
Sheet

APPENDIX 6

How To Make a Deposit or Withdrawal

Materials:

For this lesson you will need to duplicate blank deposit and withdrawal slips for the students. You may want to use an overhead projector or laminate a large sample to use as a demonstration during your lesson. Consult the following samples.

Procedure:

1. Each student should have several copies of deposit and withdrawal slips for practice.

2. Complete one or two deposits and withdrawals as a group. You may want to use the overhead projector or a large laminated copy of the slips.

Lesson: *Deposit to Account*

To make a deposit means to put in or add (+) money to your bank account. If you make a deposit, will you have less or more money? (Answer: more)

To make a deposit, use a deposit slip. (They will probably be provided by your bank.)

1. Write the date of the deposit on the slip.

2. Write your name, so the bank knows where to add the money. (You don't want the bank adding money to your friend's account by mistake.)

3. Write the amount of the deposit. How much money are you putting in (adding)?

4. Now what is your new balance? What is the total amount of money you have after you added the deposit? (You will find your old balance in your bank book.)

   Write your new balance on the deposit slip.

5. Finally, sign the deposit slip.

6. When you go to the bank, give your deposit slip and the money to the bank teller.

7. Be sure the teller gives you a receipt or stamps your book. (Don't rely on someone to ''remember'' without writing it down.)

8. Be sure all steps are complete.

Lesson: *Withdrawal from Account*

This is the same as the deposit lesson, except that you are subtracting money from the account, rather than adding it.

To make a withdrawal means to take money out or subtract (−) money from your bank account. If you make a withdrawal, will you have more or less money in the bank? (Answer: less)

To make a withdrawal, use a withdrawal slip.

Notes: When you go to figure the new balance, be sure that the students subtract the amount from their old balance to get the new balance. When the students go to the bank, be sure that the teller counts out the right amount of money that students are withdrawing.

Sample blank deposit and withdrawal forms for use in Mini-Society.

Answer key for Economics Questionnaire in Appendix 7: 1a, 2d, 3b, 4a, 5d, 6b, 7c, 8a, 9b, 10a, 11a, 12b, 13b, 14a, 15b, 16a, 17a, 18a, 19b, 20b, 21a, 22b, 23c, 24c, 25b.

APPENDIX 7

Different Approaches to Evaluating Your Mini-Society Experience

    A. Economic Objectives of a Mini-Society System

    B. Economics Questionnaire

    C. Mini-Society Mathematics Tests 1 and 2

    D. Journal Questions

A. Objectives of a Mini-Society System

After studying and experiencing concepts in Mini-Society:

1. Students will be able to recognize the dilemma of scarcity by defining its components and saying that there is not enough of everything they want.

2. Students will be able to react to the scarcity situation in their interaction–discussion group by offering tentative solutions to the problem of scarcity.

3. Students will be able to give an advantage and a disadvantage for each tentative solution to the scarcity problem.

4. Students will be able to decide upon one method for dealing with scarcity (e.g., "pay for what you want").

5. Students will be able to decide upon the activities for which they will be paid.

6. Students will decide upon the criteria for selecting civil servants to observe these activities.

   a. They will determine the types of civil servants they want (e.g., treasurer, paymasters, etc.).
   b. They will provide a rationale and priority for each criterion associated with a particular job.
   c. They will create a job application form for civil servants.

7. Students will discuss the advantages and disadvantages of various methods of submitting bids for the design of currency, and they will select one method.

   a. An individual student may submit a bid for only one denomination of currency.
   b. An individual may submit bids on as many denominations of currency as he or she wishes.

   c. Students will form into specific committees, and each committee will be assigned one denomination of currency to design. The committee will submit its best design to the government, and the entire committee will share the fee for the winning design.

8. Students will decide upon the name of their currency, the denominations of their currency, and the advantages and disadvantages of particular denominations (e.g., a nineteen-glep bill might hamper efficient exchange because of the difficult computations necessitated).

9. Students who are interested will fill out civil servant job application forms and verbalize to a committee of three why they should be hired.

10. Students hired as civil servants will disburse income to the Mini-Society citizens according to the prespecified criteria (see objectives 5 and 6).

11. One-quarter of the Mini-Society citizens, within one week of receiving currency, either will buy or sell a good or service such as felt-tip pens, erasers, tutoring services. etc.

12. By the end of one month, every citizen in the Mini-Society will have bought and/or sold a good or service.

13. By the end of one month, at least six students (assuming an average class size of thirty) will have demonstrated entrepreneurship by opening a business in accordance with the demand of the citizens (wallet-making business, bank, etc.).

   a. In a debriefing session, three characteristics of entrepreneurship will be identified by the majority of the students.

   b. At least two advantages and disadvantages of going into business for oneself versus working for others will be identified and discussed.

14. By the end of two months, each student will list at least one idea for a business venture in accordance with the demand of the citizens.

15. Students will identify the main elements of an auction and decide to participate as buyers, sellers, the auctioneer, and/or observers, listing the advantages and disadvantages of each role.

   a. At least one student will volunteer to play the role of auctioneer and show competency in the following areas:

     (1) Soliciting the items to be auctioned (at least four items).

     (2) Soliciting the minimum buying price from the potential sellers.

(3) Ascertaining whether the potential sellers want to auction the items themselves or pay a fee or percentage to the auctioneer.

(4) Providing for the recording of buyer, seller, and purchase price for each item auctioned. (This function is often performed by a civil servant.)

(5) Conducting the auction and demonstrating verbal skills including sufficient voice volume, articulation, and variation; and recognizing potential bidders.

b. At least one-third of the students will participate in the auction by making bids and/or buying items.

c. After the first auction, no more than two students will persist in bidding against themselves.

d. After the first auction, any student who bids for an item without sufficient funds will never do it again.

16. At least six more Mini-Society citizens will show, after the first auction, entrepreneurship by opening a business.

a. The citizens in business will demonstrate accounting competency by doing the following:

(1) Listing all business expenses.
(2) Listing all sales.
(3) Determining their profits.

b. The citizens in business will demonstrate advertising and merchandising competency:

(1) By verbally engaging customers.
(2) By visually creating customer interest (e.g., signs, packaging, and display).
(3) In written form (e.g., newspaper advertisements).

c. The citizens in business will devise special gimmicks to attract customers:

(1) A one-glep note inside each product.
(2) Buy two, get one free.
(3) Personalizing products using initials, etc.

17. Students will distinguish in a debriefing session between accounting profit and economic profit. They will:

a. Compute the accounting profit they are earning per week.
b. Estimate how much they could be earning per week in their next best alternative (their opportunity cost).
c. Determine whether they are in their best possible employment;

specifically they will determine whether they are making a normal profit, an economic profit, or an economic loss.

18. After a Mini-Society citizen has gone out of business or has had to lower his or her price because of a competitor selling a similar product at a lower price, students in a debriefing session will analyze the effects of competition on the selling price of the product, the producer, and the consumer by verbalizing that:

    a. The price will tend to decrease until only a normal profit remains.
    b. The consumer will pay the lowest possible price for this product.
    c. The producer will sell the product at a price that covers out-of-pocket costs but allows him or her to make enough money to stay in business.

19. After a Mini-Society citizen has gone out of business or has had to lower his or her price because another citizen has entered the industry, students in a debriefing session will analyze the effects of freedom of entry on the demand for their own product by verbalizing that:

    a. A decrease in the price of a substitute good causes a decrease in the demand for their own good.
    b. An increase in the price of a substitute good causes an increase in the demand for their good.
    c. Freedom of entry into the market tends to result in lower prices for the consumer.

20. When income increases generally in the Mini-Society, the students in a debriefing session will analyze the effect of this phenomenon on demand and price by verbalizing that:

    a. An increase in income tends to cause an increase in demand.
    b. An increase in demand tends to cause an increase in price.

21. When an advertising campaign in the Mini-Society convinces most citizens that they will be happier as a result of buying a certain product, the students in a debriefing session will analyze the effect of this phenomenon on demand and price by verbalizing that:

    a. The increase in demand is a reflection of a change in taste.
    b. The increase in demand brought about by a change in taste causes an increase in price.

22. When a Mini-Society citizen discovers that by lowering the price of a good or service the amount bought increases, the students in a debriefing session will analyze the situation by verbalizing that:

    a. This is not a change in demand.

    b. This is a movement along the demand curve.

    c. This differs from a change in demand in that it is only a change in price rather than a change in tastes, income, or price of other goods.

23. When a Mini-Society citizen has a supply of goods on hand that nobody appears to want, the students in a debriefing session will analyze the situation by verbalizing that it is to the producer's advantage to accept any price offered, regardless of the original cost of production (the concept of sunk cost).

24. After a Mini-Society citizen has observed another citizen unsuccessfully trying to pass money that is not the accepted currency of the class, the students in a debriefing session will analyze the situation by verbalizing that money has value only if it is accepted in exchange for goods and services.

25. After Mini-Society citizens have observed that their demand for goods and services is outrunning the supply of goods and services, the students in a debriefing session will analyze the situation by verbalizing that:

    a. The price of goods and services has gone up.

    b. The label for this phenomenon is *inflation*.

26. After eight to twelve weeks of Mini-Society development, the government will introduce the concept of receiving payment for its services. After the government has informed the citizens of the number of services it is rendering to them without payment, students will react to this situation by setting up an equitable tax structure that may consist of one or more of the following:

    a. Corporate income tax.

    b. Personal income tax.

    c. Property tax.

    d. Sales tax.

27. Three weeks after the imposition of a tax system in the Mini-Society, the majority of the citizens will be able to demonstrate the computational skills requisite to filling out tax forms.

Name _____ Grade _____

B. Economics Questionnaire

Directions: Circle the correct answer for each question.

1. All societies have the problem of scarcity because:
    a. the members of *every* society want more goods and services than its resources are able to provide
    b. they cannot decide the best way to provide goods and services
    c. some societies have less goods than other societies
    d. some societies have more resources than other societies

2. Choose the phrase below that does *not* represent a common economic problem
    a. what to produce
    b. how to produce
    c. for whom to produce
    d. why to produce

3. If you eat lots of candy and get lots of cavities from the candy, a *real cost* to you of eating candy is
    a. about $2.50 a pound
    b. you won't have good teeth
    c. a decrease in your dentist bill

4. Assume the Hawaiian sugar crop has failed, so that as a result the price of sugar has gone up for candy manufacturers. You observe that the price of candy bars rises everywhere in town. Which of the following is true?
    a. The quantity of candy bars demanded will be less.
    b. There will be more candy bars sold.
    c. Both of the above.

5. One benefit of competition in our economy is that it helps to
    a. increase market power
    b. decrease the number of businesses
    c. force prices up
    d. keep prices down to a reasonable level

6. When the total demand for goods is greater than the total supply of goods at current prices,
    a. prices go down
    b. this leads to inflation
    c. both of the above

7. Money is valuable because
    a. people must work to receive it

b. it represents gold and silver

c. it is accepted in exchange for goods and services

8. Linda has a difficult choice to make. At 1:30 on Saturday she can go ice-skating with her friends or see a play with her mother. What is the scarce resource?

a. time

b. money

c. skating

9. In addition to the problems of what to produce and how to produce it, a problem faced by all societies is

a. why to produce

b. for whom to produce

c. neither of the above

10. When people in business talk about the cost of producing something, they are talking about more than just their expenses. They are talking about

a. what else they could have done with their money and time

b. how much they are going to make

c. both of the above

11. Assume that saccharin and other sugar substitutes have been banned. Which of the following would happen?

a. The price of sugar would go up.

b. The price of sugar would go down.

c. There would be no effect on the price of sugar.

12. Inflation is

a. a decrease in taxes

b. more dollars chasing the same or fewer goods

c. fewer dollars chasing the same or more goods

13. In your daily lives you are constantly required to make choices because of

a. plenty

b. scarcity

c. the mean magician

d. equilibrium

14. A toy company is trying to decide whether to make cowboy belts or space helmets. Under which of the three decisions faced by all societies does this decision fall?

a. what to produce

b. how to produce

c. for whom to produce

d. none of the above

15. If the benefits to you of having a pet turtle are less than the costs,
    a. you should have a pet turtle
    b. you should not have a pet turtle
    c. you should visit a pet shop

16. Styles for women's fashions change quite often. Assume that the new styles will have longer skirts than the former styles. What do you predict will happen when women across the nation shop?
    a. The demand for longer skirts will probably go up.
    b. The demand for shorter skirts will probably go up.
    c. Both of the above.

17. When there is only one manufacturer producing an item, this is called
    a. monopoly
    b. free enterprise
    c. competition

18. Which of the following will cause an inflation?
    a. The government spends more than it receives.
    b. The citizens work harder than before.
    c. Business people try to make more profits than before.

19. The real or true value of money is
    a. the amount stamped or printed on it
    b. what it will buy
    c. what the government says it is worth

20. A producer is trying to decide whether to use machines or hard labor to package a product. Into which of the three classes of problems faced by all societies does this fall?
    a. what to produce
    b. how to produce
    c. for whom to produce

21. You bought your dad a neat model plane for his birthday and paid $40 for it. What is the *real* cost to you of buying him that gift?
    a. what else you could do with $40 plus your time
    b. $40 plus your time
    c. neither of the above

22. If you are producing popcorn to sell on Thursday, and *every* Thursday you are left with twenty-five unbought bags of popcorn, you might solve this problem by
    a. learning to make popcorn faster
    b. lowering the price of popcorn
    c. both of the above

184

23. If Greg is offering balloons for twenty cents each and Marilyn starts offering balloons for fifteen cents each, this is called
    a. monopoly
    b. unfair
    c. competition

24. The United States uses two basic types of money
    a. gold and silver
    b. barter and bargaining
    c. cash and checking accounts

25. If everyone accepted bubble gum in exchange for goods and services,
    a. bubble gum would not be money
    b. bubble gum would be money
    c. people would throw away bubble gum

Teacher: Find answer key at end of Appendix 6.

C. Mini-Society Mathematics Test 1

Name _____

1. 26
    ×7

2. 34
    −6

3. 125 − 25 =

4. 15% of 60 is

(a) 13.50   (b) 11.25   (c) 10.50   (d) 9.00

5. The chart shows the number of units that would be demanded by
    individuals at different prices. Show the quantity that would be
    demanded at each price.

Price for each unit	Quantity demanded by individuals	Total quantity demanded
$6	0, 0, 1, 1, 0	_____
$5	1, 1, 2, 2, 0	_____
$4	2, 1, 2, 3, 2	_____
$3	2, 3, 3, 4, 2	_____
$2	3, 4, 5, 4, 2	_____
$1	5, 5, 6, 5, 2	_____

Plot the points on the graph to show the quantity people would
demand at each price level.

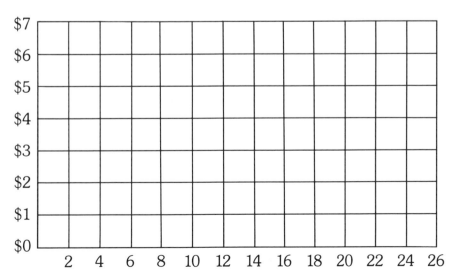

186

Mini-Society Mathematics Test 2

1. Huey has a lemonade stand. He makes four pitchers of lemonade each hour. He is open from 10 A.M. to 4 P.M. If he doesn't take time off for lunch, how many pitchers of lemonade can he make in one day?

   Answer: _____

2. The price of a new album is eight dollars. The salesclerk adds six percent sales tax to the price. What is the total price of the new album?

   Answer: _____

3. There are twenty-eight students in the class. Twenty-five of the students remembered their homework. How many students forgot their homework?

   Answer: _____

4. Someone from another country came to our town and wanted to buy one of Donna's money belts for eight dollars. The other country has a currency called bartos. The exchange rate is one dollar equals three bartos.

   a. How many bartos must the visitor pay Donna for the money belt?

   Answer: _____

   b. The visitor gave Donna thirty bartos. How much change in bartos would she give?

   Answer: _____

5. You have been selling cookies for one week and you want to know how well you are doing. Your total revenue for the week is $50. If your total cost is $45, how much profit would you have realized?

   Answer: _____

6. The graph shows how much four people sold in one day. Who sold eight dollars worth of goods that day?

   Answer: _____

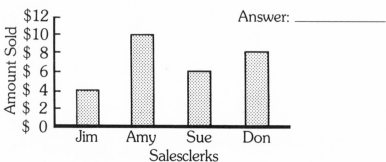

D. Journal Questions

1. List at least two instances of scarcity that you focused on or generated in your classroom.

2. List all solutions to scarcity that were discussed by your students.

3. List the agreed-upon method for dealing with scarcity in your classroom along with its advantages and disadvantages as perceived by your students.

4. List all activities for which your students chose to be paid.

5. List the civil service positions created by your students along with the job criteria for each position; include one sample of a job application form.

6. Describe what you believe were the two main attributes of the students selected as civil servants.

7. Write a brief description of the process your students followed in naming and creating their currency, country, and flag. Include physical samples.

8. Write a brief description of the methods designed by your civil servants for disbursing income to the citizens.

9. List at least four goods or services that changed hands the first week the currency was in circulation.

10. List the first six businesses that opened in your classroom in the order they opened. Write a statement about the success or failure of each.

11. What characteristics of entrepreneurship were identified by your students?

12. What were the advantages and disadvantages identified by your students of being an entrepreneur versus being an employee?

13. In your opinion, what were the three most exciting business ventures in your Mini-Society? What were the three least exciting and why?

14. Describe the first auction that took place in your classroom in terms of who participated in each of the roles, what items were auctioned and at what prices, and how records were kept. List any anecdotal occurrences.

15. Describe the last auction that took place in your classroom in terms of who participated in each of the roles, what items were auctioned and at what prices, how records were kept, and any evidences of pupil growth that occurred between the first and final auction.

16. Describe any bank, loan, or insurance activities that took place in your Mini-Society.

17. Give examples of the effects of advertising and merchandising on the success and failure of businesses in your Mini-Society.

18. Was taxation introduced in your Mini-Society? If so, describe the outcomes in terms of the types of taxes selected, how they were collected, who did the computation, and the students' reactions.

19. List all the businesses that operated at one time or another in your classroom and the approximate duration of each.

20. What were the three main noneconomic outcomes of Mini-Society activity in your classroom? Give specific examples of each (e.g., improvements in language).

21. Include a sample of one of your formal debriefing lessons.